HEALER IN HEELS

**YOU ARE THE ONE YOU HAVE BEEN WAITING FOR:
SIMPLE PRACTICES TO TRANSFORM YOUR LIFE**

HEALER IN HEELS

YOU ARE THE ONE YOU HAVE BEEN WAITING FOR: SIMPLE PRACTICES TO TRANSFORM YOUR LIFE

Jasna Burza

PANTEON PRESS
MINNEAPOLIS • FLORENCE • SARAJEVO • ROME

Illustrations by **LeAnna Wurzer**
Cover photography by **Gael Vaurin**
Interior design by **Booknook.biz**

ISBN
979-8-9882603-0-1 (paperback)
979-8-9882603-1-8 (hardcover)
979-8-9882603-2-5 (ebook)

Acclaim for
HEALER IN HEELS

Jasna has beautifully woven the wisdom from countless scientists, spiritual masters, world renowned healers, and her own life and professional experiences to provide you with a heart-based, practical and meaningful guide to heal yourself and discover how to live your best life.

—**Dr. Eva Selhub**, Author of *The Love Response*,
The Stress Management Handbook, and others

This is a book for the times.

—Former Governor **Mark Dayton**

Jasna has taken what scientists, psychologists and mystics have learned through the ages, and presents it with an intelligent and spiritual way that is weaved together beautifully, one that only she could with her soul. She has written a book that should be read by everyone. It would do our world some good.

—**Bahram Akradi**, Chairman and CEO of Life Time®

Jasna's genuine heart-felt philosophy will resonate with anyone with a pulse. Engaging and page-turning, you will learn about her childhood, growing up with the hardships of being in a war, but despite this, her mother's philosophy to 'keep calm and carry on' which was obviously a positive influence on her, and which she is now radiating outwards into the world through her work. She guides us through her encounters with people who have helped or influenced her on the journey, such as healers, philosophers, scientists and practitioners that she met along the way, each bringing a piece of the puzzle of healing and enlightenment. Her writing is completely authentic, from-the-heart, and a lived truth that resonates in every cell. I think people are going to love it and be inspired by it.

—**Gloria Prema,** author of *It's All Light:*
Juicy science meets spirituality without religion

Into our frantic and isolating world comes this powerful book, chock-full of transformative stories and scientific research, demonstrating how you—yes, you!—can be the healer of your own life. If you've felt overwhelmed or paralyzed by life's ups and downs, you're not alone. Sweet friend, help is here. Jasna's voice and spirit are what you need right now. Whether you soak up her words in one sitting or many sittings, you'll breathe a sigh of relief as she calmly shows you how to recover your joy and unmask your purpose.

—**Elissa Elliot,** author of *EVE*

There is a growing global movement to reconnect with our deepest roots. Beyond evolution, does humanity have any deeper purpose? What about a single person? What is my purpose and how do I manifest it in my own life? *Healer in Heels* responds to these questions through the lens of quantum physics. On the surface, quantum physics with its technical language and scientific concepts, is typically considered to be the territory of only the physicist. What does physics have to do with daily living? *Healer in Heels* invites the reader to see that the world of quantum physics is not just the world of the scientist but your world too.

Healer in Heels offers you the possibility to connect with the ancient wisdom and path to peace through purposeful living through a scientific paradigm that is not only for the physicist.

Jasna translated the unfamiliar and sometimes difficult concepts of Whisperology and quantum physics into a language that is accessible to anyone who wants to explore the power of living with a deeper sense of joy and purpose.

—**Steve Tonsager**, Founder of Whisperology®

The *Healer in Heels* is a portrait of a resourceful woman whose courage and conscience will be tested by violence, PTSD, and chronic sickness. Jasna Burza's life is about giving rather than trying to impress or dominate. At the same time, it isn't bland or shy. While the tone is intimate, the sweep of a vast world—from her birthplace Bosnia to Minnesota—is nonetheless palpable. One can tell right away that Jasna never had anything handed to her. Bosnia is where she learned grit. She began to understand her inner spirit and began to dig. She found what drove her. She found herself. For me, it was a method of understanding.

Jasna writes about healing herself as a *spiritual activity*. She offers credible instructions to awaken our minds to live *consciously*. They're stories, anecdotes, reminiscences, funny and sad jokes, and shared experiences. *Healer in Heels* is a friend speaking to us and letting us know it's okay. It's okay. All of it. All our neuroses and hang-ups and setbacks. We all have some PTSD in us. The question is, are we willing to take Jasna's hand and be ready to rewrite our story?

—**Dr. Nisha J. Manek**, MD, FACP, author of
Bridging Science and Spirit: The Genius of William A. Tiller's
Physics and the Promise of Information Medicine

Healer in Heels is a self discovery guide. Her ability to make connections between physics, the Universe, our inner lives and outer lives, is profound. She gives not only insights, but the tools, practices, and techniques to live our lives more fully.

—**Betsy Weiner**, Spiritual Teacher

Reading this book is like spending a few delightful hours with your wisest, kindest friend while she schools you—in the most loving way—in the art of living fully, peacefully, and with joy. Burza is a vibrant, engaging narrator, and her passion for her subject is infectious. Healer in Heels offers readers an accessible primer in the science of mindful living, and, even more importantly, the inspiration for putting that science to work in their lives.

—**Marya Hornbacher**, New York Times
bestselling author of *Wasted*, *Madness*, and others

Dedicated to every person who knows pain but continues to walk toward the light to make this world a better place. Heal one, heal all.

You are the one we have been waiting for.

Disclosure

This book is not a best seller—*yet*. This is not a marketing tactic. This sign is here to teach a principle in the book: building a quantum bridge. In the realm of quantum physics, there is something called the observer effect that explains how human observation changes the behavior of particles. Your thoughts will transform something that existed only as a possibility into something actual; they will transform an abstraction into a fact, an idea into a thing. With this sign, I am collapsing a quantum wave and I urge you to read the science behind it in Part III, starting with Chapter 6. Intriguing, isn't it?

Daydreaming pays dividends.

Table of Contents

Foreword

A Tale of Two Cities, the classic novel by Charles Dickens, begins with this famous paragraph:

> *It was the best of times, it was the worst of times, it was the age of wisdom, it was the age of foolishness, it was the epoch of belief, it was the epoch of incredulity, it was the season of Light, it was the season of Darkness, it was the spring of hope, it was the winter of despair, we had everything before us, we had nothing before us, we were all going direct to Heaven, we were all going direct the other way.*

One measure of a true classic is that its themes are universal and timeless, and it's hard to read this paragraph without thinking that it is an accurate description of our current era. We have more access to information, for better or worse, than any previous generation and just like the setting for the novel, the time of the French Revolution, we also bear witness to staggering wealth contrasted with terrible poverty. How will we manage so that rather than going "the other way" we can move toward wisdom, Light, hope, and Heaven?

A good place to begin is in the pages that follow. Jasna Burza's amazing life story is also a Tale of Two Cities. Now, with her husband and children, she lives in Minneapolis, Minnesota, a city renowned for its high quality of life. But, as a child in the war-ravaged city of Livno, Bosnia-Herzegovina, she witnessed the worst of human behavior—attempted genocide, ethnic cleansing, systematic rape, torture, and massacres of innocent civilians. The Balkans conflict in the 1990s was an appalling display of the darkness, despair and hellishness referenced by Dickens. Jasna writes, "I grew up in a war zone, lived in a refugee camp, and was raised in a time of severe economic hardship. Nothing was easy."

In this powerful book, Jasna guides you to adopt the most effective strategies for resilience and personal growth, no matter how bleak your circumstances; and she does so as a shining, inspiring example of everything she teaches.

She writes, "If we ask humans what they want the most—deep down—the answer is likely inner peace, happiness, or health. However, our actions say something different. What we do often flies directly in the face of what we want. That is because we tend to accept the world as it is and our emotions as they are without acknowledging that our thoughts and emotions are being manipulated by the outside world."

As a highly successful Life Coach, Jasna guides her clients to bridge the gap between their good intentions and their actual behavior, between great expectations and their fulfillment; and in this compelling work she shares many of her most effective methodologies that will allow you to do the same. This book offers a cornucopia of insights and practices to enrich your life. Among my favorites are Jasna's approach to cultivating and refining intentionality. I'm particularly moved by the intention statement she created for her home and her family:

"Create an environment of kindness, love, peace, and the grace of God. This house is being assisted by the Great Unseen. This is a sacred space, and people in this house flourish, increase in consciousness and know faith, possibility, and joy without doubt. And so it is. Thy will be done."

She adds, "We are not a religious family, but we do believe that a beautiful energy exists and is here to support us and lives in all of us. We call it love." Jasna embodies this consciousness of Love, and it emanates from every word in this book.

I also love the delightful Bosnian quality she introduces called *merak*. She writes, "While there is no direct translation in English, *merak* is best described as a deep desire for pleasure, joie de vivre, moments of bliss... The word likely derives from the Greek verb *meraki*—to do something with love, soul, and creativity; to put your whole self into something. Although success in life is desirable, it must never come at the expense of merak."

In other words, the *way* we achieve our goals is as important as the goals themselves.

Achievement is too often divorced from quality of life and the result isn't good for anyone. Success without fulfillment is empty, soulless. Jasna shows the way to find fulfillment and success, to achieve our goals and live beautiful, soulful lives.

She writes, "I don't believe humans are here just to go through the motions, accumulate stuff, and live mediocre lives. I believe there is a kind of genius within us all, a genius we are here to fulfill. I believe we have the chance to realize our purpose and leave this world a much better place."

Amen!

Dickens' classic ends with these words of wisdom and hope:

"I see a beautiful city and a brilliant people rising from this abyss, and, in their struggles to be truly free, in their triumphs and defeats, through long years to come, I see the evil of this time and of the previous time of which this is the natural birth, gradually making expiation for itself and wearing out."

Jasna's book also ends with words of wisdom and hope, and she includes practical guidance on what you can *actually do* to be truly free and contribute to a more beautiful world.

—Michael J. Gelb   April 21, 2023
Author of *How To Think Like Leonardo Da Vinci*

“ *That morning, as my spirit sank and I felt I could not go on, something majestic—a bright light in the darkness—seemed to catch me before I fell too far and it held me up. Something told me I was going to be okay.*

Introduction

A hot yoga class; several rows of women stood on their heads. They were thirtysomethings, flexible and sleek; their outfits matched their mats. Even upside down, they looked composed, powerful—like they belonged.

"The heat burns away the toxins and releases whatever you need to let go," came the instructor's calming voice.

Good, I thought, sweating. Exactly what I needed. Burn it all and let me start again.

She guided us through the last few asanas. As we moved into the final pose—the "happy baby"—I laid on my back, thankful no one could see me, and began to cry.

I vividly remember the first time. Three in the morning, my husband asleep. I sat on the bathroom floor, blood gushing out of me every few minutes. Strangely, that provided temporary relief. Until the contractions started again. Doctors told me the baby had stopped growing and that my body would expel the tissue. Just go home and wait, they'd said. The body knows what to do. Maybe my body knew what it was doing. I did not. Nothing had prepared me for this. Alone on the bathroom floor before dawn, unable to do anything other than bear witness to my loss, grieving what could have been a Happy Baby.

I wondered if this was some type of cosmic punishment for squeezing that little kitten in the refugee shelter when I was ten. The kitty died a week later. It must have been the kitty.

It was my fourth miscarriage. Although five more would follow it, that proved to be a turning point for me. That morning, as my spirit sank and I felt I could not go on, something majestic—a bright light in the darkness—seemed to catch me before I fell too far, and it held me up. Something told me I was going to be okay.

Looking back, I know that moment is what inspired this book.

> **SOMETHING MAJESTIC—A BRIGHT LIGHT IN THE DARKNESS—SEEMED TO CATCH ME BEFORE I FELL TOO FAR, AND IT HELD ME UP**

I was talking with a friend who was feeling overwhelmed with life ever since the pandemic—school shootings, war, inflation, and a pervasive sense of uncertainty and anxiety seemed to rule her days. "I just don't know what's wrong with me," she said. "I'm not myself anymore." Already on anti-anxiety medication, she felt the need to up the dosage, but even that, she feared, wouldn't help. "I'm losing my mind," she said, defeated. "Nothing is working."

What she didn't know was that I had been hearing some version of this daily—from friends, colleagues, and clients. It wasn't just her. It was all of us. The pandemic shifted something in us; we are all fundamentally different, in one way or another. Most of the people I talk to are experiencing an overwhelming sense of restlessness.

Among the symptoms that characterize post-pandemic syndrome are over-the-top anxiety, irritability, excessive drinking, overdependence on electronics, physical agitation and restlessness, feeling overwhelmed, overscheduling, fragmented attention, difficulty relating, blaming and judging, poor attention to needs (including those of children, partners, and ourselves), heightened sense of self-righteousness, sleep disturbances, fatigue, frequent physical ailments, and depression.

A recent study by a team of investigators from Harvard Medical School and Massachusetts General Hospital and published in *Brain, Behavior, and Immunity*[1] found that many Americans have experienced a sharp uptick in these symptoms since the pandemic. "[The] severity and/or prevalence of symptoms of psychological distress have increased considerably in the United States since the pandemic onset (CDC, 2020; Abbott, 2021). Likewise, an increased prevalence of fatigue, dyscognition (i.e., "brainfog") and other symptoms has been reported, including among the non-infected," the study reports. The study also explores how preliminary research suggests that for some uninfected individuals, societal and lifestyle disruptions during the COVID-19 pandemic may have triggered brain inflammation that could affect mental health.

Populations around the world have been on the road to feeling overwhelmed for some time; the pandemic exacerbated that pattern and the resulting distress. Almost immediately, with the emergence of the COVID-19 virus in late 2019, the sheer confusion of a historic global health crisis generated a level of chaos, pain, and sense of being overwhelmed that no one could have predicted. We all felt it—the weight of the world on our shoulders, the suffocating pressure of being caught up in something bigger than ourselves, something both dangerous and amorphous, whose nature we didn't even know.

However, as we move ahead, we need to heal. We need to overcome the lingering anxiety of that time and find ways to

AS WE MOVE AHEAD, WE NEED TO HEAL

grow as individuals and as a collective. We must learn how to live with our worries instead of letting them control us. We must take a step back from the chaos and make a space of stillness for ourselves in the world again.

---

1. Brusaferria, L., et al. (2022). The pandemic brain: Neuroinflammation in non-infected individuals during the COVID-19 pandemic. *Brain, Behavior, and Immunity, 102*, 89-97.

We are not crazy. There is a reason for this restlessness, these mental disturbances and a spiritual malaise. On top of these factors, the incessant noise brought to us through social media and our phones means that we have been plugged in more than ever. As a result, we are unable to tend to the issues arising around mental and spiritual health. However, these issues have secrets to teach us and could be an opportunity to completely reshape our lives and those of everyone around us.

This is an opportunity to pause. It is a chance to re-examine our lives. As Socrates famously said, the unexamined life is not worth living. Examining our lives often means facing uncomfortable truths we may have avoided for a long time. We may now encounter aspects we've pushed away, buried, or numbed. Now we have the opportunity to address those aspects and heal the parts of ourselves that have been neglected far too long.

If we ask humans what they want the most—deep down—the answer is likely inner peace, happiness, or health. However, our actions say something different. What we do often flies directly in the face of what we want. That is because we tend to accept the world as it is and our emotions as they are without acknowledging that our thoughts and emotions are being manipulated by the outside world. Right now, we are experiencing collective anxiety and fear—powerful and persuasive emotions that drive human beings to make very different choices than they might in times of balance and peace.

I have so much compassion for all of us. I am fully aware of how difficult it is to become conscious and intentional, to reject the habits and addictions to which we've all become accustomed, even as we try to navigate the rough waters of life in the modern world. Society molds us and demands that we show up a certain way—and we do, often-

IN ORDER TO CHANGE OUR OWN LIVES, WE MUST BELIEVE WE CAN

times sacrificing the things that matter most. That sacrifice will ultimately be too great; but in order to change our own lives, we must believe we can.

There has never been a better time to change the direction of your life. When we've already lost so much, what's at stake? We stand to gain an enormous amount of peace, stability, and joy in this process of transformation and change. What have we got to lose?

Life brings challenges to us all. Some spread slowly through our lives, like a crack in the foundation of who we are, or thought we were; some are swift and sudden and seem certain to destroy us all at once. Often these moments of crisis are also moments of transformation and change. I've come to believe that these transformative moments create an opportunity, however unwelcome, for us to respond. Although, too often we react, avoid, or ignore the possibility inherent in these liminal spaces in our lives. Weakened by pain and exhausted by loss, we turn away from the heat of the fire that could burn away what we can no longer use and make us into the more powerful beings we could become. We reach for something that will distract us, numb us, lessen the immediate experience of pain.

Obviously, in the long term, this is more harmful. It costs us: we lose what insight we might have gained, and we miss the opportunity to become stronger and more prepared for the next challenge. I witness this sort of paralysis happening on a mass scale right now.

I understand. I tried to do the same thing. Even though I knew my loss had changed me, I didn't fully embrace the gifts it had to offer, the wisdom it was meant to bring.

In 2018, I traveled back to Bosnia, where I was born, after a 20-year absence. Upon arriving in my home country, my heart began to pound—not with excitement but with terror, a fear more powerful than I have ever before felt. My husband and two small children had traveled with me because my father was dying of cancer. My husband knew right away something wasn't right. "Are you okay?" he asked. I didn't know how to answer. I just knew I couldn't breathe, and I felt like screaming. I wanted to jump out of my own skin.

Shortly after returning to the States, I was told that I'd experienced a delayed onset of post-traumatic stress disorder (PTSD). I came to the U.S. with such wide-eyed optimism and hope for a better life that I never looked back; the horrors of my childhood were in the past, and I wanted them to stay there. Why would anyone invite the kind of pain those memories would bring? Look at this great country with such abundance and freedom! I was a kid in a candy store. However, the body keeps the score, and at the height of my career and adult success, it was as if I'd been swept away by a rogue wave. In fact, I was being dragged under by the riptide of my past. I was living in constant fear, remembering with visceral power the horrors of shelling, gun violence, bombing, and hiding in shelters. I remembered violence; never feeling safe, internally or externally; and never feeling like I mattered. The miscarriages were painful, but the return trip to Bosnia shattered my entire world.

I called my sister and told her that I must be severely ill because I felt like a different person every day. My mood swung all day long, careening from normal to hyper-vigilant to terrified and back again. I'd get up in the middle of the night to make sure the house was locked, repeatedly. If my kids screamed or dropped toys, I'd panic. I'd hide in the bathroom just to avoid the noise.

I knew I had to listen. I knew that panic had something to teach me. I knew this wasn't me and that something was wrong. Furthermore, because of my professional background, I knew I needed to shine a light on it because that kind of internal chaos—like the principle of chaos itself—will eventually take over if left unchecked. I read books; I sought out coaches and healers; I went on walks; I slept a lot; I did all types of meditations and tried all types of healing modalities; and eventually, I was able to find my way home.

Nothing about that time was easy. But it was necessary. By walking through it, rather than running away, I was transformed.

There is a before and after to my life. I believe this kind of transformation is available to all of us, especially in these trying times. In fact, I believe the discomfort we're feeling right now is exactly the call we need to heed; it's telling us it's time. We need to go on this journey.

We all know deep inside there is this voice we cannot explain. A sense of awe. An awareness of the presence of guidance. Many of us have forgotten to listen, and the clamor of the world makes it hard to hear.

WE ALL KNOW DEEP INSIDE THERE IS THIS VOICE WE CANNOT EXPLAIN

I don't believe humans are here just to go through the motions, accumulate stuff, and live mediocre lives. I believe there is a kind of genius within us all, a genius we are here to fulfill. I believe we have the chance to realize our purpose and leave this world a much better place. However, right now, caught up as we are in this global simulation of reality, this video-game version of life, we are drunk, asleep, and unaware of the potential we possess. The answer is to heal all parts of ourselves and access our genius. In the words of Walter Russell, "Mediocrity is self-inflicted. Genius is self-bestowed."

"MEDIOCRITY IS SELF-INFLICTED. GENIUS IS SELF-BESTOWED."

This book is a spiritual primer for this day and age, a treatise for these trying times and our practical-minded souls. You can read this book in one sitting, be inspired, and glean some interesting information; or you can finally let it be the book that changes everything. Even the first practice I suggest, in which you'll learn to create coherency and tune out the world's chatter, will give you results. However, imagine if you took the next step, and the next. Imagine if, instead of making another list of things you want to achieve in the new year, you commit to a paradigm shift, to a way of being that changes how you experience the world and, as a result, changes the world.

Science now bears out what mystics have believed for millennia: as Rumi wrote, we are the universe in ecstatic motion. We are the

WE ARE THE CREATIVE FORCE IN THE UNIVERSE creative force in the universe. Every breath, thought, and action creates a ripple effect from the microcosm of our little lives to the macrocosm of the cosmos itself.

You need never open a physics textbook to harness the power of physics in practical ways. How do I make my day better? How can I be more productive? How do I ground myself in this world? Science offers answers to these questions, and the tools to put them to use are within our reach.

In this book, I'll offer a few of the practical tools I use—all of them backed by science, readily available, and tried and true—as well as the insights of individuals who've shared their wisdom with me. Their experiences, like my own, show that it's possible to create peace and harmony in our inner lives even as we acknowledge the harshness of the outer world. I am neither aloof to nor ignorant of that world. On the contrary, my awareness of it convinces me even more strongly that we must learn how to protect our energy, cultivate and heighten our vibration, and, in doing so, create positive changes in the lives of the people around us and in the world.

Everything I will share; I have learned along the way. Some of these things will resonate deeply with you; others won't. I'm not a guru, and this book does not offer a simple prescription for fixing your life. I am a fellow traveler. This book's

THERE IS NO ONE WAY; THERE IS ONLY *YOUR* WAY purpose is to point out the possibilities available to all of us and to serve as a practical companion on the way. There is no one way; there is only *your* way.

Your way to healing, purpose, joy, and abundance will make itself known through those things that resonate the most with you. These will be the things that bring you joy, that feel right and true. However, if you intend to find your own path and walk it, you have to take the first step, to decide and to believe that it is possible.

My intention for this book is to provide you with the spiritual inspiration and practical resources to live your life in a new way. I especially hope that it can serve as a form of a reset, a reflection point, an honest rendezvous with yourself. When you look at yourself in the mirror, I want you to feel safe and strong enough to admit how you feel, what you want, and who you are, and to take your first steps toward healing—physically, emotionally, mentally, and spiritually. I believe we are all due for a reset, one that will allow us to look deep within and understand that we have guidance every step of the way.

By incorporating simple, effective daily practices, you can create a meaningful life. For me, the process of incorporating one practice after another, testing each one for myself, has changed the entire quality and trajectory of my life. These are the practices to which I return every time I lose my temper, lose a clear sense of myself, or become swept up in the world's chaos. These practices become so habitual and easy, they're second nature, like adding a little salt to your dinner when it's lacking something. Over time, you'll know instinctively when to add a touch of salt and how much.

In the pages that follow, you will learn a practical, proven approach for applying the power of quantum physics, holistic healing, and positive psychology into your everyday life. You will learn how to tune out the noise of the world, bring body and mind into balance to increase your vibration, deepen the peace you carry within and your connection to the world without, and awaken the healing potential you possess.

We are at a crucial moment in history: We have the power to change this collective experience. As a species, we're heading straight for a brick wall, but no one wants to hit the brakes because then we'd have to admit we're out of control. If we admit that, then we must start healing; and healing takes work—and time.

The answers for which we've been searching are already within us; we are the healers we seek. We are the ones we have been waiting for.

How to Use This Book

If you are feeling overwhelmed and all over the place, this book will help you ground and find inner coherence. If you want to learn to create consciously, learning about the field of potentiality will show you how to turn your dreams into actuality. If you are whole and aligned and want to take it to the next level, you will find yourself in the chapters on activating genius and creating something for the good of others and the greater good. Some of this may seem akin to magic; but as scientist Dean Radin says, "Magic doesn't mean 'no cause.' It just means that we haven't yet developed scientifically acceptable theories to explain these effects."[2] Again, the only way to know is to test this for yourself.

You can watch *Spartans* on TV all you want—you still won't attain the level of discipline and strength you admire until you do what they do. Action is the antithesis of fear. The process of transforming the self requires discipline, self-awareness, and the willingness to overcome challenges, but more than anything else, it requires persistence. If we want to see change, we must get up every day and take concrete action toward that change again, even when we want to least. It's a curious fact that some of our greatest accomplishments

---

2. Radin, D. (2018). *Real Magic: Ancient Wisdom, Modern Science, and a Guide to the Secret Power of the Universe.* Harmony.

are directly preceded by some form of hardship. Transformation does not necessarily require pain, but it does require work. Maybe that's the magic—maybe showing up for ourselves and what we want, every day, is what creates the change.

Years ago, when I was teaching yoga, I used to say, "Transformation happens at the edge." Right at the point of that uncomfortable asana, if we stay just a few breaths longer, we find that it doesn't break us; instead, it breaks through the resistance that prevents us from moving on. For example, I used to absolutely hate the chair pose; my teacher told me that was precisely the pose I needed to do repeatedly. This is a stark contrast to the culture of comfort we have created for ourselves. In the process of sticking with things, we honor the ancient Greek aphorism, "know thyself," which is more closely translated as "know your measure." When we create the space to explore the spaciousness and limits of the mind and body, and take the time to reflect and observe, we can do so with a clarity that often seems hard to find.

If all you do is read this book and put it back on the shelf, it will not give you the change you want. It's by doing the work, most notably writing and reflecting, that the transformation can be achieved. Commit to small increments of time to transform yourself; this is the most rewarding investment you can make. So, grab a special journal that will only be associated with this work, something that will be pleasing to your eye, and you will come to associate it with your journey to "know thyself." Let it be a guide, a companion, and a teacher for years to come. Write down ideas and insights as they come to you. Whatever you do, take the time for you to cultivate the connection to yourself and the *field* (I will explain this), which will tell you secrets, offer guidance, and infuse life with a peace many of us never thought possible. Maybe it's just an extra 20 minutes in the morning before everyone wakes up. Turning all electronics off an hour before sleep and being present to the moment. Fight for these moments because they are sacred, important, and the quality of your life depends on them. As I write this, harp music is playing, candles are lit all around me. I pray that the love and peacefulness of this very moment permeates the moment you read this, and by the time you read this book, you will know that it is so. You will have walked the path and we meet here. And so it is.

PART

COHERENCE

Imagine a lazy Susan turning really fast in the center of a table, covered with Lego pieces for the car you are building. To build the car, you need to get a lay of the land, look at the instructions, and then find the individual pieces that fit. But how do we do that when the lazy Susan keeps spinning so fast it's making you dizzy?

That's what the world and our lives feel like right now. Everything is spinning at such a pace that it feels like we can never slow down or catch up. We're trying to grab the pieces we need to create the lives we want, but because everything's spinning, we keep grabbing the wrong ones, or they end up flying off the darn thing and then you can't find them, or the whole thing breaks. This, in physics, is known as chaos or entropy. The same principle applies to our lives, our bodies, and our minds. If things are chaotic, it affects ALL aspects of our lives negatively. It's difficult to slow down and breathe when that happens because our fight-or-flight mechanisms have been activated, and in fact, seem to be on high alert all the time.

So much of our culture is telling us that if we just *try*, we can keep up with the spinning and maybe even get ahead, we can somehow grab the right pieces to create the lives we want from the scattered array of responsibilities, tasks, and dreams, saying, *Come on, you can do it!* in this annoying cheerleader-y voice that sets us up for failure and makes us feel we aren't good enough. But we must stop the spinning first. Then, and only then, we can identify the pieces we want or need. From that place of greater order, we can intentionally create something that's our own.

This is where physics comes in. In this section, we'll be exploring the concept of coherence as an antidote to our chaotic lives, a force that can actively counter the sense of chaos and feeling overwhelmed and we can bring our lives into alignment and order. I define coherence as alignment with oneself, the environment, and one's reason for being here. Coherence translates into our lives as clarity, organization, and focus; a sense of effortlessness; an ease of creative expression; a state of flow. When we are in coherence, we are walking in step with the laws of the universe. You know those days where you simply seem to flow through your day and you're humming your way through the list of things that need to be done? That's coherence. When you are in that state, you're cohering all systems of self toward wholeness.

Coherence is the opposite of chaos; in scientific terms, it is negentropy. Before we begin to work truly on ourselves and build something great, we must come into a place of coherence within ourselves. The first step is to escape the mainstream, retreat a bit so we can organize, cohere, and then fortify. At that point, we can decide how to move forward.

This is the first step on this journey, and it's a vital one; jumping ahead only leads to exhaustion, disappointment, and lack of fulfillment. All chapters are written in a way to set you up for success. If you do only one thing, focus on coherence. To cohere all systems toward wholeness requires only a few simple steps that don't cost anything but your intention and time. You don't need an app or a gadget or another course. You just need to begin, pick one thing at a time to attend to. You also have a manual to return to every time you lose a sense of your alignment, your coherence.

Regardless of who you are and what your role is in this world, you are a healer, a person capable of making yourself whole. This is a way of describing our ability to heal all parts of ourselves, regardless of how we look or who we are, and without delegating our power to the few who we deem worthy to be healers. Heal one; heal all.

CHAPTER 1

You Are a Healer

Tending my inner garden went splendidly this past winter. Suddenly to be healed again and aware that the very ground of my being—my mind and spirit—was given time and space in which to go on growing; and there came from my heart a radiance I had not felt so strongly for a long time.

—Rainer Maria Rilke

A Most Unusual Healer

I was greeted by a beautiful blonde woman who sent me to the treatment room to wait for Steve, the healer I'd traveled to see. I settled in on the massage table, wondering what this session was going to be all about.

I had been to so many healers and therapists and providers and acupuncturists, and at this point, I really didn't know what else to do. After my return to Bosnia for the first time in 20 years and the delayed onset of PTSD, allergies I had as a child returned to plague me. I would wake up in the middle of the night with bleeding arms because I was itching so hard. It seemed like everything I ate was a trigger. I would clutch my handbag when walking down the street, check if my house was locked multiple times in the middle of the night and more often than that, check to see if my kids were breathing.

Well, that wasn't very convenient. I was 37 years old and living my best life. I couldn't possibly have a nervous breakdown. I was the happiest person I knew. What on earth was happening? But as they say, the body keeps the score; mine never forgot, and it knew I was finally safe enough to deal with this.

I firmly believe that to help others, you need to be integrous in what you are teaching and preaching to others. As a life coach, I felt like I couldn't serve my clients. So, I closed my practice, and I started to walk. Every day. I walked and walked and walked. I listened to Deepak Chopra and Greg Braden and Wayne Dyer and Lynne McTaggart and Joe Dispenza and David Hawkins—all of these wonderful souls who wrote about pain and purpose and consciousness.

By the time I went to see Steve, I had improved. I'd waited eight months to see this man. My mental health was back to its "normal" at this point, but the allergies were still a concern. After so many futile attempts to heal myself, I was ready to try again.

Looking back, I had been healing all along. With every walk and

LOOKING BACK, I HAD BEEN HEALING ALL ALONG

every book and every new piece of information, I was healing. By the time I met Steve, the world's most unusual healer, I was ready not only to heal but also to learn.

Steve asked me just a few questions, then told me he didn't need to know more. He grabbed my ankles and moved his hands over them, explaining that he was testing me. Well, that was weird. But I had done so many weird healing sessions at that point that I was just willing to do whatever. Most of the session was silent; he did not speak. He just kept waggling my ankles and moving his hands, and I got a chance to look at the ceiling tiles and contemplate. Then, a sudden surge of energy flowed through my entire body. I felt as if I literally floated off that table. I was flooded with an expansive sense of love, joy, and relief, a feeling of total wellbeing that I hadn't felt in a very, very long time. I started to cry tears of happiness. I had never taken drugs, but it seemed like that feeling must be what it meant to be high. The sensation lasted for a while. The only word I can use to describe it is bliss.

I felt radically different after that one session. The skin issues went away overnight. What kind of magic was this? I had a million questions for this unusual healer. It was very clear that he was not interested in sharing his techniques in that initial meeting. But I couldn't stop asking my questions. What on earth did he do? How did he do it? What modalities did he use? How was it possible that he fixed the things in my physical body that no one else could address by identifying something about shame and pride? I wanted to know it all. Steve told me there was no need for me to come back. I knew that as well. But I needed to understand so I could tell others, so I scheduled a follow-up appointment without any need for subsequent healing.

I returned for several more sessions, arriving each time with new questions. My brain, mind, and soul were all hungry for answers. Session by session, he would assign me homework and books to read and research to do. And I did. Every single time.

Much of what I learned made sense; there were rational, scientific, and commonly accepted explanations for the effects this healing achieved. However, there were also things that deeply resonated with me even though I knew people would call me crazy for believing. I have come to know that almost all of us experience profound and unexplained things. Many of us believe in God without any scientific proof. We just believe. An interesting thing happens when

**THE WORLD WE LIVE IN
NOW REQUIRES A LITTLE
BIT MORE BLIND FAITH**

it comes to healing: we laugh at others for their blind faith that they can change the trajectory of their life or illness, even as we claim to believe in a dude who walked on water. That is one powerful cognitive dissonance. However, the world we live in now requires a little bit more blind faith—not in religion so much as in our own potential and ability to transform our lives.

Thus began my education in the power of quantum physics, quantum mechanics, thermodynamics, non-local healing, intention research, kinesiology, and the whole vast range of scientific research that informs this work and explains why I healed along with thousands of other people Steve has treated. My skin allergies went away, but I was profoundly a different person in numerous ways. Something inside of my heart shifted, which I now know is the most profound way of healing and a place from which the physical manifestations originate.

I read every book I could get my hands on in the hopes that I could integrate the emerging science of consciousness and spirituality with my knowledge of what healing is and how it works. As fascinating as science truly is, my hope was and is to make it accessible, practical, and available to anyone. In this book, I'll explain how quantum physics has helped people, often without them being aware of it, and how it can help you tap into the power of physics in practical ways that can assist you in leading a more aligned and happier life.

Quantum mechanics is the branch of physics that explores the very small world of particles at the atomic and subatomic level. In many ways, quantum mechanics challenges our understanding of reality and how we perceive the world around us. Every advance in this branch of scientific discovery brings us deeper into the unknown, strengthening the connection between science and spirituality, and suggesting there is far more to reality than what we can see or fully understand. I am not a scientist and do not claim to be one. However, I do want to share with you the implications of this research.

You are a healer

The people we meet on our journeys often turn out to be teachers like Steve. This single person changed the course of not only my healing but also my life. My meetings with Steve sent me on the journey to discover for myself much of what you are reading in this book—the title of which captures an important experience I had studying with Steve. He taught me the principles I needed to know; I would implement them in practical ways in my daily life, and then I would come to him for help again. He kept saying, you are a healer, you can do it. Although, is a life coach who wears fancy dresses and heels *really* a healer?

I had a misconception about what and who a healer is, how he or she dresses or behaves. Yes, I love spirituality and meditation, and yes, I hug trees and am able to influence my energy and heal myself, but I'm also spicy, and I love business and fashion—and somehow, I couldn't reconcile all these aspects. Steve started calling me the Healer in Heels and it stuck. I *am* a healer in heels.

You too are a healer, just as you are today. This is a way of describing our ability to heal all parts of

> YOU TOO ARE A HEALER, JUST AS YOU ARE TODAY

ourselves, regardless of how we look or who we are, and without delegating our power to the few who we deem worthy to be healers. Steve taught me that I am the one I have been waiting for. The more I sought his guidance, the more he urged me to listen to the guidance within. The more I asked about healing, the more he affirmed my ability to heal myself and others. Heal one; heal all.

Whisperology®

Stories of miraculous physical healing abound, but we don't know much about it. I used to think most people were skeptical of the idea, but new research conducted by Barna[3] found that most Americans believe in supernatural physical healing—a whopping 66 percent. Furthermore, more than one quarter of Americans claim to have experienced a miraculous physical healing. These powerful statistics make me wonder what people who experience healing have in common, given that they come from all faiths and backgrounds, including many being atheists or naturalists. My experience with healing suggests that it's not just physical; though my skin issues went away after a single session with a gifted healer, it was the mental aspects of my being that experienced the most radical shift. I was a different person. Isn't that healing? I have come to find that it is. Healing the inner is foundational in healing the outer, a principle that manifests in so many ways for all of us.

My healer, Steve, started his practice a few decades ago. Trained as biochemist, toxicologist, clergy member, and acupuncturist, he was always deeply rooted in his Christian faith and he was interested in the intersection of consciousness and spirituality. His practice was intended both to provide clinical care and to apply some of the things he believed could heal but for which he had no proof. He formed a friendship with Stanford professor William Tiller, who spent decades researching intention (you'll learn more about Tiller's work through my conversations with Dr. Nisha Manek, who worked with him as well). Steve and his wife Ardith were both profoundly interested in the connection between spirit, consciousness, and physical healing. I have talked to numerous people who experienced miraculous healing in his care, from cancer remission to infections

---

3. Barna Group. (2016, September 29). *Most Americans believe in supernatural healing.* Barna Group. https://www.barna.com/research/americans-believe-supernatural-healing/

clearing overnight and resolving a range of autoimmune diseases. He did this through something he called Whisperology, something that would become a huge part of my life.

What on earth is Whisperology?

Whisperology is an informational system based on spiritual principles that uses Intention Based Field Resonance Testing (IBFRT) to receive and send coherent information for healing and spiritual growth. In Whisperology, coherence refers to the alignment of the body, heart, and mind to its divine origin and purpose, which is based on the belief that we experience optimum health when we seek to love God, others, and ourselves in our daily living. Even though I am not religious, this concept appealed to me especially because of its clear foundations in science. As a life coach who spent over a decade helping others find their purpose, what further intrigued me was the emphasis on purpose as being foundational to healing.

Steve says,

> Whisperology is based on the understanding that life is thoroughly purposeful down to the last detail. As spiritual beings, the greatest source of fulfillment is alignment with a divine purpose. My belief is that when there is alignment with a spiritual purpose, what was lost within us has been found. When we wake up to the deepest meaning in our lives, there can be true freedom and transformation. Every level and layer of our being, physical and non-physical, is intended to serve this intrinsic purpose. All IBFRT methodologies are framed within a spiritual context. Coherence brings health on every level. This is the message that is at the heart of Whisperology.

TO HAVE OPTIMAL HEALTH IS TO BECOME ALIGNED WITH ONESELF AND ONE'S PURPOSE

To have optimal health is to become aligned with oneself and one's purpose. This is what it means to become whole. To use your time here for a purpose that is meaningful and fulfilling, to be aligned and coherent. This is the ideal; but we live in a world where it's becoming increasingly more difficult to do any of these things.

How Whisperology works

To explain Whisperology, Steve uses the analogy of a house: If we asked what a house was, we would recite parts of the house (e.g., roof, walls), similar to our body and separate organs. However, we then must ask that if we don't have people or tools to assemble the house, do we have a house? So, would we have the body if we don't have mechanisms that make organs flow and connect—the energy systems and raw materials that make the cells? We have to ask: How do the workers know how to build a house without a plan or a blueprint? They don't; they start with a blueprint for that house. In the same way, we don't have a person without a blueprint for that person—it's more than just DNA. Whisperology works to restore the blueprint, which is now referred to as information medicine.

Whisperology uses the power of intention to activate health on all levels. It's a reverent, gentle, and peaceful exchange of information and energy with the body, not a medical treatment. It's a whisper, a prayer, a specifically healing and loving intention for the person needing healing. You might ask, how in the world can an intentional whisper change my allergies? Well, the allergy is just a manifestation of something far deeper; Whisperology listens to that and seeks to heal us there.

Another helpful metaphor is to think about computers: When there are problems in our lives, they are similar to the way a virus from an email can infect and corrupt separate programs and eventually the whole operating system. It could be mild—just slowing us down a little—or it could be more severe. To repair the programs the virus affected, we must not only delete the virus, but also upgrade, reinstall, or reset. The same happens with our bodies: We need to not just treat the virus but also go deeper.

Whisperology holds that the origin of incoherence is in the informational field, so only by treating that realm can we restore what is being manifested in the physical. Incoherence can be physical, emotional, mental, or spiritual. Spiritual incoherence means that, consciously or unconsciously, we are not aligned with our purpose for being here. As such, life will not bring about inner satisfaction. Whisperology's ultimate goal is to align us with our purpose for being here, thus eliminating major incoherencies that lead to the gradual destruction of our being.

Steve's explanation of Whisperology immediately brought me back to the time of my miscarriages and the sea of physical ailments I experienced. The pain forced me to surrender, reassess, and change course. Quitting the corporate rat race and starting my own life coaching practice was life changing on all levels: it brought coherence to my life, a sense of purpose, service, alignment, and joy. Within months, all physical ailments disappeared, after years of treating them to no effect. Soon after, I gave birth to two children within 14 months. The wrong job and misaligned purpose brought existential distress that manifested physically in my body. Treating the body alone alleviated symptoms temporarily, only for them to resurface not much later. It was only by going deeper, much deeper, that I could heal those parts of myself. Instead of Band-Aids, I had to go to the source of the dis-ease in every aspect of my being.

Our actions and experiences leave a mark on our informational pattern, our blueprint. The more misaligned we are, the more incoherent we become, which means that our energy fields become equally chaotic and destructive. That creates an incredible amount of stress that eventually manifests in our physical body. So, the key is to return to the source of it all.

How you can use the power of Whisperology in your life

Much of what Steve told me affirmed what I already knew; some of what he said opened my eyes to even more possibilities. He never promoted his work, and he didn't claim to heal anyone. He fully understands that the power to heal is accessible to all of us, should we choose to accept it.

Here are just a few things Steve has taught me that have shifted the way I look at the world. I hope they will be of assistance to you as well.

- We don't find peace by controlling the world. The gifts of the spirit come from within. We labor under the false belief that we can secure happiness by acquiring things, when it is accessible only through grace, surrender, and the journey into oneself. Most of our life is spent trying to control outcomes and circumstances, but the effort gives us only a false sense of security. True security resides within; it can be found in stillness, reverence, and letting go. This is why we talk about tuning out the noise, going within, and reconnecting to ourselves.
- Thoughts have energy, just like information has energy. Every thought and word we utter has an informational quality to it; as such, we can use thoughts and words to create change. Thoughts, whether spoken or held in the mind, can be beneficial and creative or destructive. They define our worlds. Steve echoes David Hawkins, a widely known author and teacher in the fields of consciousness and spirituality, that we are subject to what we hold in mind. I knew my thoughts and words were powerful, but it was only on this journey that I realized their

true power and the physics behind it: Thoughts turn to things. Studies show us that thought changes physical matter, the behavior of atoms. What are we made of? What is everything else made of?

- Some spaces have different qualities than others. Holy places are "conditioned spaces" that have been infused with special properties through the power of intention. "Conditioned space" is a term that William Tiller coined. Steve utilized Tiller's research in his healing spaces. This is why I felt the immediate sense of peace in Steve's healing room: It was a space blessed with prayer many times, a space of surrender and humility. It carried a wave of peacefulness and love, which felt like a warm hug when in distress.

- There is a connection between attention and intention. We have to pay positive attention to things in our life to create an energetic force to counter the power of negative attention. We're not denying the existence of negative things, but rather refocusing consciously to focus on those things that nurture us spiritually and allow us to be kind. As attention follows intention, we tend to create these positive emotional states in our lives through our actions. From Steve, I learned to do this through the drills he has created, which are a form of intentional meditation and, more importantly, a tool for self-healing on all levels. These drills are included in his books, which can be found on his website.[4] A recorded version of the drills is also available for download on my website.[5]

---

4. www.whisperology.com
5. www.jasnaburza.com/healerinheels

The 80/20 rule

I developed the 80/20 rule for myself as I started to teach and coach struggling entrepreneurs. We're taught that to attain success, we have to go all out, working nonstop, always "hustling." For years, I prided myself on this approach. As an immigrant, especially, my favorite saying was, "I will outwork anyone." The need to prove myself worthy of being here and to show that I could compete in American life was so strong that I forgot many beautiful aspects of my culture, like the "merak" feeling of bliss after a small cup of coffee or moment of sunshine. I forgot that feeling because I came to a place that glorified hard work, so I obliged happily. I still work hard, and I love my work, but I no longer allow it to come at the expense of my health or my time with my family.

Many evenings, when I plug in my phone to be recharged for the following day, I realize that I haven't recharged myself. We spend the majority of our time on anything *but* those things that will help us find coherence and joy: meditation, prayer, walks in nature, and stillness. Yet, these are the things that will give us everything we want. During my journey, when not much was at stake for me professionally, I started to play with this idea of spending the vast majority of my time, 80 percent, in alignment

I STARTED TO PLAY WITH THIS IDEA OF SPENDING THE VAST MAJORITY OF MY TIME, 80 PERCENT, IN ALIGNMENT

ment, doing the things that bring me into coherence: walks, good sleep, time with kids, reading, praying, writing, intending, dancing, gazing out the window, and admiring the beauty of the natural world. The rest of the time I would show up ready to work and be of service recharged. Interestingly, everything went better when I did this. The 80/20 rule isn't a perfect percentage of time spent; it's a rule of thumb that keeps me mindful of what matters most. I still work 10-hour days when I see clients and I love those days, but I still wake up before dawn and pray, write, and send healing intentions to others.

I sought Steve's help because of my skin issues that no one seemed to know how to address. The doctors just gave me more steroids. Through my work with Whisperology, the skin issues and allergies were resolved, but the most remarkable gift was that I found a way home. I remembered who I was and what I came to do.

I now understand that painful moments serve as a wake-up call for us all. I listened to that call, and I am so glad I did; I have learned to hear the whispers that are there to guide me home.

Exercise: What is part of your 80/20 rule?

Remember, this is not an exact percentage of time spent, but more like an energetic focus. What are the things that fall into that category of recharging yourself that will bring you into alignment? It's important to note that this differs for everyone, but when you have that list, you have clarity about your needs to be your best. Do you need to run, dance, or take long walks or baths? You will be surprised how much more energy you have to do the things in your life when you give yourself the things that bring you into alignment.

Merak is your birthright

In Bosnia, where I was born, people prioritize something called *merak*. While there is no direct translation in English, merak is best described as a deep desire for pleasure, joie de vivre, moments of bliss. Bosnians insist on having it daily, starting with their coffee ritual, which happens multiple times a day. *Oh, this is merak,* one might say with satisfaction and appreciation for the beauty of the moment.

MERAKI—TO DO SOME-
THING WITH LOVE,
SOUL, AND CREATIVITY;
TO PUT YOUR WHOLE
SELF INTO SOMETHING

Children observe adults doing this, and soon they too understand the meaning and importance of merak and continue the practice. The word likely derives from the Greek verb *meraki*—to do something with love, soul, and creativity; to put your whole self into something. Although success in life is desirable, it must never come at the expense of merak. In the United States, a great deal of value is placed on material success, money, and fame. Striving after these things is validated, and we are praised for the effort we put into achieving them, even when that effort includes punishing practices and comes at great cost to our personal lives. Our environment and our culture all influence values, priorities, choices, and goals; there is no objective measure of what matters, what has meaning, what has worth. So, it is up to us to decide what we truly want, what we are willing to do to get that, and what we are willing to let go.

Let me give you an example; when I first started my business, I wanted to be successful and well-known. I loved what I did, but I was driven by a desire to be successful, to achieve the American dream so others would see me as successful, to prove myself once and for all that I was worth investing in. What did I mean by success? Success according to whom? I defined it according to what I saw—successful coaches and inspirational figures who sat on the couch with Oprah, dispensing their version of wisdom and expertise. For a long time, anything less than that meant I still wasn't good enough.

After I started to incorporate some of these practices, that changed. I gave myself a stamp of approval, a stamp of worthiness. I feel content, happy, and successful because I changed my definition of what success meant. I didn't need to be seen or recognized as successful according to others; therefore, the exhausting, endless striving stopped. I still have goals and aspirations, but they are based on different values, and the energy to work toward them comes from a different place. I would love to meet Oprah—not be on her show, if she still had one, but to be in her energy, to admire her trees, to pick produce in her garden, and to discuss with her how I used to watch her show in Bosnia. The impulse is different—it's about my respect for a woman I admire, not about what meeting her would get me.

In 50 years or so, I will no longer be on this planet. What will I do with the time I have been given? What kind of life do I want to live? The answer is simple: I want the life I'm living right now. So, I start living from that vantage point and understand the impermanence of everything the mystics have been discussing for millennia.

The kind of world most of us live in has us running on a hamster wheel, chasing after something new, something better. It's a system that rewards striving with more striving, want with more want, and it trains us to believe there is never enough. It's not a formula for joy. So, what if we start with joy?

Exercise: What is your merak?

What moments in your life put you in that state of bliss, full enjoyment of life, and feel luxurious and fulfilling? Make a list of these moments and intentionally make time for them.

Be-Do-Have

This is a popular framework I teach to help my clients introduce change. It provides us an insight into three ways for trying to obtain what we want.

Most people believe they need to *have* something before they can begin to create change. They tell themselves first they need more time, more money, better health, or a different house, and *then* they will be happy and successful. The problem is they don't have these things; therefore, they're constantly waiting for circumstances to change so they can do and be what they want to do and be.

Another pitfall is starting with a *do* variable. These people are focused on doing more, telling themselves that once they do this and finish that and learn this and start that and resolve the other thing, *then* they'll be satisfied; but the more they do, the more they become defined by doing, and soon they are exhausted and burned out. They may do what they set out to do, but it's never enough; there's always more to be done, and the cycle continues.

There is a third way of approaching change, and it is the underlying concept of this book. It's not about what I want to do or have but who I need to *be*. This isn't about changing the exterior factors in our lives; it's about an internal change, a change of identity that James Clear, in his book *Atomic Habits*, outlines beautifully.

First, decide who you want to be. This whole than any level—as an individual, as a team, as a community, as a nation. What do you want to stand for? What are your principles and values? Who do you wish to become? Ask yourself, "Who is the type of person that could get the outcome I wanted?" And, "Who is the type of person who could lose 40 pounds? Who is the type of person that could learn a new language? Who is the type of person who could run a successful startup?"[6]

> **"WHO IS THE TYPE OF PERSON THAT COULD GET THE OUTCOME I WANTED?"**

He discusses choosing who you want to be as the prerequisite and motivating force for the actions you will take, which then become powerful habits. I love this approach—and it works.

---

6. Clear, J. (2018). *Atomic Habits: An Easy and Proven Way to Build Good Habits and Break Bad Ones*. Avery.

It doesn't mean we don't *do;* it just means that our doing is aligned with who we are, and our actions become a natural and positive extension of us. To become more coherent in mind, body, and spirit, there are a host of physical components that need to become aligned. So, for example, if you want to lose weight, coherence will help your mood, sleep, and schedule. You may not drastically restrict your food intake or force yourself to move your body because when you are in a coherent state, your body naturally finds homeostasis, of which healthy weight is just one measure. Each desire we have is led by our own inner state. Changing our state means the desires that do not align with who we really are no longer drive us.

Many of these practices focus on learning how to be present in the midst of an experience that may be unpleasant or uncomfortable. As a starting point, let's remember that the goal is not to change the experience—which is not within our control—but to change how we feel about the experience, which most certainly is.

However, when we're overwhelmed with life in general, how do we even begin to take charge? We begin by identifying one aspect of our lives where we want to make a change, committing to take the action required to change it and following through.

Many of us struggle to believe that things such as "joy" and "happiness" are attainable. We become cynical. This is called cognitive immunization, a process of rejecting facts that conflict with our deeply held beliefs. It's why we dig in our heels when those beliefs are questioned, and we find ourselves defending a part of our lives that makes us unhappy or an aspect of our behavior that keeps us stuck. This neither serves us nor helps us to create the best version of ourselves. Unfortunately, sometimes things have to get painful enough for us to be willing to do something about them. Fortunately, we don't have to wait for pain to become willing. We can simply start at the place of discomfort.

Hope is the magic elixir

Faith is the substance of things hoped for, the conviction of things not seen.

—Hebrews 11:1

Hope—blind faith without any proof—is the magic elixir. Why? Faith affords you the courage to put one foot in front of the other when you otherwise wouldn't. It serves as the light in the darkness. A good friend of mine, Huldah, told me about the time her husband asked her for a divorce while she was pregnant with their second child. She said, "I'll never forget this one moment." Huldah continued,

> In the midst of my marriage falling apart, I was stuck in traffic in D.C. and talking to my then-mother-in-law, and a thought came to me and I said it out loud, through tears: "I know my life is going to be amazing because I'll be in it." I didn't even totally get where that self-assurance came from, but once I said those words, I felt so damn comforted. Life was still painful and hard, but I found this inner strength that I couldn't fully explain.

Huldah went on to create a wonderful life for herself, and she healed along the way. But it was that moment of determination, hope, intention, and faith that changed something inside of her. That's how powerful this process is.

Regardless of who you are and what your role is in this world, you are a healer, a person capable of making yourself whole. That healer can be accessed through the practices I will

REGARDLESS OF WHO YOU ARE AND WHAT YOUR ROLE IS IN THIS WORLD, YOU ARE A HEALER, A PERSON CAPABLE OF MAKING YOURSELF WHOLE

introduce. When we are an open channel, allowing that source energy to flow through us, not only are we healing ourselves but we are also healing others and the world. Think of how we use electricity: We might not understand it, but we use it every day. As Marya Hornbacher wrote in her memoir *Wasted:* "Healing requires one thing above all: it takes action. This will not be done for you. Eventually you, yourself, will have to choose how to do it, how to live. You will have to find your way."[7]

Exercise: Be-do-have

What is something that you really want that seems elusive? Instead of thinking about that external goal, think about who you want to *be*. What sort of person can get the outcome you want? Who would you *be* if you had everything you wanted? You are that person; now is the time to focus on the assets and skills you already possess. Write about what those are and how they can help you on your journey to achieving your goals, both without and within.

7. Hornbacher, M. (1999). *Wasted: A Memoir of Anorexia and Bulimia.* Harper.

"Stepping away from the world is also a step toward self-healing, a way to process trauma, grief, and loss so that we can return into our lives with more clarity than ever before. We can then choose what steps we take to create a new, more desirable reality with purpose and intention.

2

Tune Out the Noise: Coherence

Silence is the sea, and speech is like the river. The sea is seeking you: don't seek the river. Don't turn your head away from the signs offered by the sea.

—Rumi

Years ago, I met with a wonderful client whose schedule overwhelmed her. She was building her business and trying to fulfill all of life's responsibilities, and on top of that, she had to chauffeur her kids to what seemed like a million different activities for which she'd sign them up. I asked her, why did you sign them up for all of those things? She said, "Isn't that what everyone does? All of their friends have millions of activities, enrichment events, and sports. All I want to do is give them the best future possible, the future that I didn't have." I knew where she was coming from; she wanted to give them opportunities to explore and expose them to various experiences. However, the end result was that she was stressed out and overwhelmed—and so were her kids. She was an incredible mother and a wonderful human, but she felt like she was falling short in every area of her life because she'd created an impossible situation; she had set herself up for failure. Her kids were exhausted and edgy; they wanted to quit the sports teams and walk away from all of the activities for which she'd paid so much money. At this point, she was just pushing ahead with the plans she'd made without questioning the effect on her or her family. Everyone was suffering—the kids, her husband, her business, and her.

She was following advice she'd been given and doing what she thought was best for her kids. However, she was also caught up in the modern-day version of keeping up with the Joneses, and no one was happy with the result. So, we took the time to question the premise. I asked her what was most important in her life. She said her marriage; her physical and mental wellbeing; and healthy, happy children. Based on what she really valued, her schedule clearly didn't align with what she wanted the most.

Most people feel helpless and cannot see a way out of the spirals in which they exist. Their commitments overwhelm them, but they find it almost impossible to walk away from any of them, let alone all. Walking away from commitments is never easy, even when we know many of those commitments aren't really satisfying to us but are things that we're doing to satisfy other people's expectations, whether of specific individuals or societal pressures as a whole. We internalize and respond to those expectations on a daily basis, often without being aware of doing so; and that's precisely why it's important to question why we do what we do. Ultimately, if we are not happy and our actions and behaviors are destroying our mental and physical wellbeing, our relationships, and our work, then we know it's not worth it. The first step is to question it, to pause, simplify, and to remove everything that is bringing stress.

Many people tell me they cannot eliminate anything from their lives. They insist I just don't understand—they simply cannot reduce their commitments or gain any control over their hectic schedules and overwhelming lives. That is not true. If we're really honest with ourselves, there are changes we could make, commitments we could let go, responsibilities that aren't really ours; making even a few of those changes could radically improve the quality of our lives.

IF WE'RE REALLY HONEST WITH OURSELVES, THERE ARE CHANGES WE COULD MAKE

My client and I devised a plan to slow things down, clear out the schedule, and cut back on the kids' activities for just one week. When that week had passed, I received a call.

"We are here sitting in the backyard," she said, the happiness audible in her voice. "The kids are swimming in the pool and having the time of their lives, I am reading and working on my business, the sun is shining, and the kids just told me that this is the best day ever. Why on earth did I drive them around town for eight hours straight? Thank you so much. I didn't realize I was in control of my schedule and the harmony in my home."

You, too, are in control of your schedule and the harmony in your home. However, first we have to tune out the noise so we can hear clearly the voice from within telling us what we want and need the most.

YOU, TOO, ARE IN CONTROL OF YOUR SCHEDULE AND THE HARMONY IN YOUR HOME

Incoherence is the state of not holding or sticking together; entropy is a lack of order and predictability. In the contemporary world, the incessant influx of information results in our minds (and often our bodies) being scattered and fragmented. We feel incoherent, out of order, unable to predict or control ourselves or our lives. The task, then, is to take steps to change the things that create incoherence and entropy in our lives.

INCOHERENCE IS THE STATE OF NOT HOLDING OR STICKING TOGETHER; ENTROPY IS A LACK OF ORDER AND PREDICTABILITY

We can take hold of the tide of information, control the sources of stress, and induce greater peace and alignment in our everyday lives.

Exercise: Stop overcommitting

Overscheduling is a sure sign that you are doing something for someone else. This is not to say that you should stop helping your friends, family members, or strangers in need—but be aware of the difference between helping others and overcommitting yourself because it will make you feel like a better person. Do your kids really need another playdate? Are your clients really going to suffer if their website isn't updated today? When we overschedule ourselves, we can feel like our lives are out of control. This can lead to feeling overwhelmed and stressed. To get back in control of your schedule, take some time each week (or even day) to reflect on what's important in your life and how you want to spend your time.

One of the main complaints of modern society is that we are inundated with information from all sides. I once read that we receive more information in one day than people did in one year back in the 1800s. It's a lot. Our brains, unable to process so much information (much of it in the form of a dopamine hit), doesn't have time to restore and return to balance; the effect is mental and physical incoherence and entropy.

It comes down to physics

Too much information and input create a mental and psychic overload, an internal form of chaos and incoherence. Physicists also refer to this as entropy: the measure of the disorder in the universe. Science describes entropy as an erosion of structure due to loss of information, resulting in disorder and chaos. I prefer to use the word incoherence because it makes more sense to me. In physics, incoherence is defined as light waves having a different frequency, length, and phase.

CHAOTIC LIVES AFFECT US ON ALL LEVELS—PHYSICAL, MENTAL, AND SPIRITUAL

Chaotic lives affect us on all levels—physical, mental, and spiritual. In the end, the only way to counteract the force of chaos is through the imposition of order—but not just any kind of order. It must be a conscious order that arises from within you as a response. When we are in a state of overwhelm, we become less effective and productive in all areas of our lives. We may feel physically exhausted or drained, and emotionally disheartened by all that needs to be done. It's not that the information itself is bad; it's just that we can't process it all at once. When we let too many things into our lives without making conscious choices about them, we end up with an overload of stuff; that stuff takes away from our available energy and our clarity, both of which we need to make conscious decisions about what really matters to us in life. When I'm feeling like I won't be able to get through the day because everything is too much and I just don't have the energy to move forward, I know I need a reset. Just like our computer sometimes needs a reboot after having 30 tabs open, our minds and bodies sometimes need to do the same. Continuing to press on through feeling overwhelmed—as if we can gain clarity by force—will cause our inner computer to crash.

We do not need another app to help us manage the unmanageable excess of our schedules and to fragment further our already-fragmented attention spans. Rather, we need what's called in physics terminology, negentropy—a force that gathers information and creates order. It's a state in which energy flows freely through systems without dissipation or degradation. In our lives, this manifests as what's often described as "flow," or being "in the zone." In direct contrast to the sense of being frazzled, stressed, and in a million places at once, this is experienced as an increase in the ability to focus, concentrate, and create, and it contributes to our overall quality of life in the form of greater vitality, passion, and excitement.

For those of us who have become acclimated to high levels of baseline stress and a constant feeling that we're doing a million things at once and none of them well, the idea of clarity and focus may seem both unattainable and maybe even—counterintuitively—a little

Exercise: Close open loops

On any given day, I have about 50 things I am thinking about: emails to send, bills to pay, kid activities to schedule, laundry to do, family members to check in with—the list goes on and on. The majority of these things are unfinished projects that infiltrate my mind like pests, nagging at my attention and pulling me away from what I want and need to do. These are "open loops"—we all have them, and they take up a disproportionate amount of our mental capacity, thereby reducing the mental space we have for anything else. It makes us feel like Sisyphus, endlessly rolling the boulder up the hill only to watch it roll down, so we have to begin again. These loops are exhausting; they prevent us from being in the moment, and, like a computer virus, they draw much energy and slow down all our other processes. One of the fastest ways to alleviate this is to do a brain dump. Write down all the things that are nagging at you, day in and day out: to-dos and responsibilities and maybes. Then, choose one or two to tackle first—don't worry about the rest until those are done. Even closing a few open loops will make you feel accomplished and quiet the incessant chatter of your mind.

scary. That's understandable; chaos and incoherence have become our norm. However, we need more than ever to create this type of coherence and peace in our lives. To do that, we first have to step back from the chaotic environment and nonstop informational input that create incoherence in our lives.

That state also comes to many of us through the practice of meditation, something that Bob Roth, an American Transcendental Meditation teacher and author, affirmed so beautifully when I spoke to him about it. Bob is one of the most experienced Transcendental Meditation teachers in the world. I have been aware of his work for years now and found great insight in his book *Strength in Stillness*.[8] As both a

---

8. Roth, B. (2018). *Strength in Stillness: The Power of Transcendental Meditation.* Simon & Schuster.

teacher and CEO of the David Lynch Foundation, Bob has dedicated his life to bringing Transcendental Meditation to millions of people, from household names like Jerry Seinfeld, Oprah Winfrey, and Katy Perry to students in underserved schools, veterans dealing with PTSD, and women and children who have survived domestic violence.

Speaking about coherence, Bob told me,

> The deeper part of the ocean is a state of complete resonance, complete harmony, complete coherence, complete peace. It's the state of pure flow, the deepest levels of nature functioning. And when we subjectively experience that in meditation, we have that pure coherence and our whole body reflects that. Our breathing is very soft. The electrical activity in our brain lines up, it becomes synchronous, everything comes into a flow.

Gloria Prema, author of *It's all Light*,[9] put it this way:

> Coherence is very powerful. An example of partial emphasis coherence would be a laser, and we know how powerful lasers are. Professor William Tiller, Department of Materials Science at Stanford University, has spent decades investigating intention and intuition and the relevance of coherence in these processes. In speaking about coherent wave patterns and the potential this creates, he uses the example of a 100-watt light bulb. As the photons are emitted from the bulb, they cancel each other out in a process known as "destructive interference"; in other words, the waves cancel each other out so you never see the full potential of the light bulb. But if you could somehow orchestrate the movement of the photons to come out "in phase" or coherent, the energy density from the

---

9. Prema, G. (2022). *It's All Light: Juicy Science Meets Spirituality Without Religion.* Independently Published.

bulb would be between 1,000 and 1 million times that of the sun! If love is indeed expressed by coherent light waves, then what does this tell us about human potential?

Incoherence shows up physically and non-physically. Any kind of chronic issues that keep pestering you are the clearest forms of incoherence. On the non-physical side, incoherence manifests in emotional states that don't feel good: feeling lost, bored, or engulfed in negative feelings. Another sign of incoherence is projecting your emotional states onto others and blaming them as the source of your pain. If we do that, it's likely we are incoherent in those moments.

INCOHERENCE MANIFESTS IN EMOTIONAL STATES THAT DON'T FEEL GOOD

We are almost never going to be in full alignment and coherence in our lives unless we have become enlightened. The more coherent we become, the better equipped we are for handling life, but we can't expect there won't be moments of distress or feeling rattled or lost. We can expect that there *will*. When we are in coherence and our expectations are realistically aligned with life as it is, we can proceed with the knowledge that a) we have been here before and we learned from what happened, and b) we can course-correct by using the tools we've acquired, including those outlined in this book.

Tune out the noise

The noise in our modern day lives comes from both information overload and life responsibilities. We have to learn to tune it out. Everything we consume makes an imprint on our lives and our minds. Although there are many ways to police our own consumption, the sheer volume of the noise in our lives calls for a more radical, direct approach: stepping away from it

EVERYTHING WE CONSUME MAKES AN IMPRINT ON OUR LIVES AND OUR MINDS

all for a period to regain our sense of grounding and coherence. The damage created by allowing the noise to rule our thoughts, feelings, and lives is real: Not only does our incoherence harm us, it brings us crashing into the incoherence that rules so many other people's lives as well. This becomes a critical mass of chaos, tearing through our health, work, and relationships, and leaving a path of destruction in its wake. Our mental health often suffers most of all because we are stripped of the capacity to achieve our potential and live full, and fulfilling, lives.

Technology has changed every aspect of our lives, and in many instances, made them better. For example, the ability to see my mom in Europe through video calling brings me joy. This wasn't possible when I first came to this country, and I am grateful that now it is. However, the global spread of technology and our ever-increasing reliance on it in every area of our lives also has undeniably negative effects. One of those is the sheer volume of information we take in, though our brains aren't capable of processing it all. There is a name for it: *infobesity*,[10] described as, "the condition of continually consuming large amounts of information, especially when this has a negative effect on a person's well-being and ability to concentrate." It's also called information anxiety or information overwhelm, and it's characterized by "the tendency to crave and digest information even when this isn't always necessary or effective for our needs."[11] This information epidemic alone accounts for the vast majority of the stress, feeling of being overwhelmed, and anxiety in people I meet.

If you are sick and tired of talking about how much we use our phones, so am I. I am also sick of people preaching about disconnecting. That said, it's a hard-cold truth that we must do so. In her book *Dopamine Nation*, Anna Lembke writes, "The smartphone is the modern-day hypodermic needle, delivering digital dopamine 24/7 for a wired generation. As such we've all become vulnerable

---

10. Macmillan Dictionary. (n.d.). *Infobesity*. https://www.macmillandictionary.com/buzzword/entries/infobesity.html
11. Ibid.

to compulsive overconsumption."[12] This overconsumption directly leads to physical and mental stress, suffering, and pain.

To find contentment, slow down our brain wiring, and avoid suffering, we need to keep our dopamine in check. According to Lemke's research, pleasure is always followed by pain. The solution? Do something physically challenging that will give you a natural release of dopamine and correct the dopamine imbalance non-stop screen time creates. Strenuous exercise, a cold plunge, or intermittent fasting are just a few examples.

As someone who grew up in dire circumstances, I always appreciated working hard and I believe that bumps along the road make me stronger and build my self-esteem. I fear that we are getting too comfortable in all aspects of our lives when we are actually designed for work—building, creating, pushing ahead. Although it may seem counterintuitive, we work hard to make life easier for ourselves, to increase our level of comfort—those same comforts, when we indulge in them too much, deprive us of happiness and actually create more suffering than ease.

When we are overwhelmed, we have difficulty making decisions and thinking clearly. We feel stuck and have trouble moving forward with our lives. We may even feel like giving up or shutting down completely. We have more than enough to do but are so overloaded we don't know how to prioritize or where to begin. Most importantly, in this vicious loop, we never achieve our full potential because of the damage to our physical and mental health.

I approach it like this: Social media, technology, all of the gadgets, and all of the opportunities these things create are there for me to use, but I need to be discerning about how I use them. I have to have discipline in my life. When I do, I find myself in control of, rather than being controlled by, the influence of the outside world on my inner peace.

12. Lembke, A. (2021). *Dopamine Nation: Finding Balance in the Age of Indulgence*. Dutton.

Exercise: Tune out world affairs

Step away from social media for just a few days. Stop listening to anything or anyone who has the intent of making you feel afraid or anxious. We are what we consume. Clean your mental diet. If you have been feeling rattled, anxious, or angry, consider the past 48 hours and see what you have been consuming, thinking, and saying. We are what we think. If we don't make the time for our brains to pause and reset, we consume the information we are given without question, which then becomes our truth. Turn off the TV and stop engaging with anyone interested in fearful or hateful language. You might ask, then how will I know what's going on in the world? Well, if something important happens, someone will tell you about it. To stay sane, I walk away from the noise and read the most wonderful books. I create space in my life to listen to what my soul and intuition tell me to do. Whatever happens in the world, I can live through it; it is up to me whether I do so in a state of fear, anger, or peace. The only thing over which I have control is my response; and only if I respond from a place of peace can I contribute that peace, at the quantum level, to the workings of the world.

"Gotta-gotta" mind run amok

Meditation has been a huge part of my life. I have not always been consistent with my practice, but I know that my day and my life are always better when I am. We've all heard about the benefits of meditation, and many of us keep meaning to start or return to a meditation practice, but the very same thing that makes us need mindfulness so badly is exactly what gets in our way. How are we supposed to find time to sit quietly with our thoughts when there is so much to do?

Bob Roth calls this incessant chatter the "gotta-gotta" mind. In *Strength in Stillness*, he writes,

What holds us back? Any number of things: Exhaustion. Foggy brain. A shortage of good ideas. Or maybe we don't know what to do, where to start. You can fill in the blanks there for yourself. The point is that meditating gives direct access to your own innermost, unbounded self. In doing so, it gives your body the deep rest it needs to eliminate the buildup of stress and tension that drains energy and undermines health. It makes available the clarity of thinking, the free flow of creative ideas and the conviction of purpose to create changes in your life and your world.[13]

I asked Bob what he advises in times like these, when the world feels out of control and our mental health seems to be seriously deteriorating. His response gave me pause.

"THIS IS NOT REALLY ABOUT MENTAL HEALTH" This is not really about mental health. If you were asked to carry a 1,000-pound block and you hurt your back, you wouldn't say that's an issue of physical health; you'd say it's too heavy. Human beings weren't made to be able to carry that 1,000-pound weight. In the same way, our mind and heart are affected by too much: the pressure, the demand, the 24/7 social media, political and social upheaval, and the economy. What we are experiencing is a natural response to something that's too much—like hurting your back is a natural response to carrying something too heavy.

I know for myself that sometimes the simple act of meditation can lift that heaviness. However, in particularly trying times, I have found it necessary to cultivate other practices because meditation alone wasn't enough. Tuning out the noise and gaining coherence require

---

13. Roth, B. (2018). *Strength in Stillness: The Power of Transcendental Meditation.* Simon & Schuster.

more than just mindfulness and meditation; we have to adjust other areas of our life, as well.

"We have to look into strengthening our back," Bob told me, "but also maybe not carry so much weight in the same way. We have to look into strengthening our brain, and that's where meditation comes in. But we also have to look very carefully at what we're trying to do. And I think we're trying to do too much."

All of us are feeling the "too much" in addition to the "gotta-gotta" mind. Today, we're dealing with the "gotta-gotta" mind run amok. The solution lies in managing those things we can control—and that means not just meditating but prioritizing and cutting back.

Bob acknowledges,

No one wants to hear that. But the reality is that if someone goes to a heart doctor and they had a near heart attack and the doctor says, "You have to cut back on what you're doing," no one wants to hear that, but they may have to. So, first we should do everything we can to transcend, eat healthy, all of that. And then, if it's still too much, we have to look into adjusting our priorities.

Hearing him say those words felt so af-firming, so down to earth, so practical and to the point. We are not crazy and it's not just us—it's *all* of us. This is a global crisis of coherence, not of individual mental health. We can't separate mental health from our physical health or spiritual wellbeing. Damage or disturbance in one of these areas causes a cascade of damage in the others, too.

> **WE ARE NOT CRAZY AND IT'S NOT JUST US—IT'S *ALL* OF US**

Exercise: Narrow your "circle of control"

In *The 7 Habits of Highly Effective People*, Stephen Covey coined the terms "the circle of influence" and "the circle of concern."[14] The circle of concern encompasses the things we care or worry about but may not have control over: government decisions, the weather, the media, and economy, among others. The circle of influence (also called the circle of control) are the things over which we do have control, such as our attitudes, decisions, actions, and perspectives. You can use the model of drawing out the two circles or simply making two lists on a piece of paper: things I have control of and things I don't. When you've separated the two, write about the things you'll need to surrender and how you'll go about doing so.

Do you have an inner alarm?

So, how do I know when it is time for me to step back from my work, my commitments, my relationships so that I can recharge and regain an appropriate perspective on things? Each of us has a different symptom, or what I call an inner alarm, that tells us something isn't right. Some of us can handle more conflict and pressure than others can. Some of us naturally have more energy than others do, but for the most part, we all know when we are not at our best. If we know how we feel and what we can do when we *are* at our best, it's easier to identify it quickly when we're *not*. From there, we can create a map for ourselves, one that shows us when we're in the clear and doing well, when we're starting to lose perspective and lose our way, when we're headed for the danger zone, and what to do if we're already there.

Here's how I know: I start being impatient with my kids. Kids are magical, and their innocent minds and brains work in such

---

14. Covey, S. (2020). *7 Habits of Highly Effective People: 30ᵗʰ Anniversary Edition*. Simon & Schuster.

beautiful ways. Unlike adults, they never intentionally want to piss me off. They are just exploring the world, testing the boundaries, and learning through play. So, when I find them in the kitchen with oats all over the floor and a mess everywhere when I have to be somewhere in 10 minutes and I lose my patience, I know I'm off. They were trying to help mama by attempting to prepare the oats for me; I'm the one who lost perspective and stepped out of line, not them. That's not who I am. So, that's when I know I need a reset. If I don't give myself that reset, I will tear through my day (and everyone else's) like a tornado, leaving a path of destruction in my wake.

When I am in a good state of mind and highly coherent, I can handle it all without too much difficulty. The oats will be cleaned up, the kids will feel good having tried to help mama, the drivers in front of me will be blessed when they are slowing me down and maybe even give me a moment to collect myself before I get to my destination.

Let's be clear—I still lose my cool, but then realize I was wrong. When you push and push and rush and rush, you are bound to explode at some point. The more attuned I become to the warning signs, the better able I am to stay in alignment and keep walking my intended path.

WHEN YOU PUSH AND PUSH AND RUSH AND RUSH, YOU ARE BOUND TO EXPLODE AT SOME POINT

In an interview I did with Dr. Nisha Manek, a physician, author, educator, and health coach, she provides these simple instructions:

> You drop your awareness down to the center of your heart and stay there. Breathe in and out and stay there. And you can repeat a single contemplative line. I am free. I am love. I am awareness. There are many others, but you can go there and just be there. And that's extremely powerful. Take a deep breath, close your eyes to the outside world and just go in.

Breathe and drop your awareness to your heart. It's speaking the truth to you. That's all it is.[15]

If we do that enough, we come into the state of transcendence. Bob Roth, who has made it his life's work to help people access that state through Transcendental Meditation, said to me:

When we get in those states and become coherent, the light will shine through all the portals. Same light. It just expresses itself. Oh, now it is in the heart area, now it's in the brain area, now it's in the immune system area. The same coherence. And that's that beauty of Transcendental Meditation: getting to that deepest level where we clear the mind, bring peace to the heart, and bring resilience to the nervous system.

Few things are more powerful than inertia, herding, and the pressures of conformity. When you're in a vast sea of bodies and souls all moving in one direction, it's hard to chart your course. However, if you exit the mainstream, if you ditch the prevailing current, then you can move forward with the swiftness and certainty of a speedboat on a placid sea.

IDENTIFY WHAT'S OPPRESSING YOU, AND ESCAPE/NEUTRALIZE IT. THE VERY FIRST STEP IS TO TUNE OUT THE NOISE.

We have to escape a trap that's partially of our own making, partially imposed on us by our culture of conformity. Identify what's oppressing you, and escape/neutralize it. The very first step is to tune out the noise.

---

15. Burza, J. (n.d.). *Uplevel together: Interview with Dr. Nisha Manek.* https://jasnaburza.com/condition-your-home-to-feel-like-westminster-abbey-with-nisha-manek/

Our environment matters

Tuning out the noise doesn't apply only to information, news, and activities. Physical clutter creates a level of chaos and incoherence that directly affects our state of mind (and in later chapters, you will learn why and how to "condition" your spaces), particularly our ability to focus, concentrate, and be productive. This is not news; the socials are full of organizing and decluttering experts and influencers, but too often we watch these programs without implementing what they suggest. Our spaces are full of information; physical clutter creates visual noise, which in turn creates incoherence in ourselves. The first step is to observe your surroundings and start decluttering slowly and deliberately.

Begin by focusing on one area—for example, the kitchen. Look around and ask yourself: Is this space organized? Does it make sense to me? Do I know where things are, or do I have to hunt for them? Are there things that should be thrown away or recycled? If so, get rid of them immediately. Eliminate anything that doesn't add value to your life. This includes stuff like old magazines and newspapers, clothing you never wear anymore, food past its expiration date, and so on. Next, take a close look at what's left and decide what needs to be organized better so that it makes sense for you. Keep in mind that you don't have to get rid of everything at once; just work on one area and then move on to the next. As you declutter your physical space, you'll notice that

ELIMINATE ANYTHING THAT DOESN'T ADD VALUE TO YOUR LIFE

you're also decluttering your mind. You'll have fewer distractions to deal with and more clarity of thought. You'll be able to focus better, think clearer, and be much more productive at work.

Practice discernment like Leonardo Da Vinci

Michael Gelb wrote about the noise and the fog nearly a quarter century ago in his book *How to Think Like Leonardo Da Vinci*,[16] and things seem even worse now. Why? In our conversation, he referenced Charles Dickens' line, "It was the best of times, it was the worst of times," emphasizing that in fact, this is neither—but it is important for us to increase our discernment and become more intentional about how we curate our lives.

Michael says,

> So, we're at the worst of times in the sense that technology has created a situation where your nervous system can easily be hijacked, and you won't get it back. [It's easy to become] addicted to all of the lowest common denominator garbage that is available on your device, and you can just get caught in everything that preys on your fear, your prejudice, your lust, your desires, without uplifting you or reminding you of who you are or what your potential or capacity is. At the same time, you [could] listen to multiple versions of Nessun Dorma sung by different singers for free instantaneously, while drinking two different great wines that you had shipped to your house at unbelievably low prices, while tasting incredible food that also was just shipped to your house and made organically in some incredible way by artisanal people who imbued it with incredible love. So, it's the best of times and the worst of times. What it requires more than ever is discernment and discipline. And unfortunately, you're not going to learn those in school. You're not going to learn those on television. You have to be like a martial artist of the mind in terms of curating what comes into your space on every level.

16. Gelb, M. (2000). *How to Think Like Leonardo Da Vinci*. Penguin.

Exercise: Create a #stopitlist using discernment

Before we can begin to add any constructive practices in our lives, we first must take the time to stop doing the things that are robbing us of our lives. What are the things you truly don't have to consume or in which you don't have to participate? Do you really have to make muffins for your neighborhood association if you haven't had a good night's sleep in days? Do you really have to watch the entire new season of *The Crown* the moment it drops? Before we continue with other practices, first we have to identify the things that are already creating incoherence in our bodies and environments. By tuning out the outside noise, we can exhale, and for the first time in a long time, ask ourselves what we really want. Stepping away from the world allows us to regain perspective, to look at our life with a wider lens. It's a lens that allows us to see what we're attracting, what we're avoiding, and whether there are other options. Stepping away from the world is also a step toward self-healing, a way to process trauma, grief, and loss so that we can return to our lives with more clarity than ever before. We can then choose what steps we take to create a new, more desirable reality with purpose and intention.

> STEPPING AWAY FROM THE WORLD IS ALSO A STEP TOWARD SELF-HEALING

Simplify your life

Time for an inconvenient truth: Most of us spend more time updating and charging our phones than we do on updating and charging ourselves. Another inconvenient truth: Most of us spend more time buying into and supporting other people's dreams than we do on creating and building our own. Pulling back for a time forces us to slow down and work on our inner selves. Taking the time away from the noise and responsibilities calls for our ability to see: to integrate things we have learned, to become self-aware, to reflect and process. Few things done

FEW THINGS DONE WITH EXCELLENCE ARE BETTER THAN MANY DONE IN HASTE AND WITH-OUT INTENTION with excellence are better than many done in haste and without intention.

I remember being in a state of over-whelm all too well. When I realized that it was getting increasingly worse, I gave myself time to rest and reflect—and cut back. What was the first thing to go? Happy hour. The combination of alcohol that never felt good the next day, and neither did spending time with colleagues complaining about our bosses and focusing on the problem. Friends are there to help you in hard times, sure, but the negativity was overwhelming. (We see this all the time—someone mentions a horrible thing that happened in the neighborhood or on the news, and people start jumping in to share something even worse. Our bodies and minds don't need that; even the act of listening to or observing a negative situation causes an observable physical response in the form of decreased strength.) So, I started there. I started meeting with friends over a walk or morning coffee; that provided the connection I wanted but imbued it with positive energy, which immediately began to improve my mood.

I also made sure that I got enough sleep every night. Research shows that every known mental disturbance is correlated with poor sleep. I stopped bringing my phone into my bedroom, and I did something called "reverse alarm": about 90 minutes before bed, my alarm goes off, and it's time to shut down my phone. I light the candles, dim the lights, start cleaning up, get the kids and myself ready for bed, and read something lovely for my soul right before sleep. Wayne Dyer, an author and speaker in the field of self-development, talked extensively about the importance of what you go to bed with at night because the thoughts and insights you have at that time will permeate the subconscious for the next 6-8 hours. If you watch a horror movie right before going to bed, how peaceful do you suppose your dreams will be? The subconscious needs time to process the day. By shutting off all input before bed, we allow the brain to slow down and relax.

What can you simplify in your life that will have a positive impact for you?

We're carrying too much; we need to put down some of this. In fact, it's imperative we do so because we are destroying our nervous system, something more precious than any amount of success or money. Bob Roth compares our nervous system to a million-dollar car:

> We would take such good care of that car. Everybody would. The best gasoline, the best tune-up. When we have a nervous system and a brain that's worth an infinite amount of money, we have to take the best possible care of it. We have to cut back, and everybody has to use their own inner common sense, [listen to] their own inner voice. What should I cut back on? What should I do less of? Everybody has to decide for themselves. And what you decide today may be different in six months or a year. But you have to be true to yourself, asking, "What do I need? What do I need to change?"

Deep down, we all know. We know what feels good and what doesn't. The more important question is: are we willing to do the work, including taking the actions that will reveal themselves as necessary in this process of discernment.

DEEP DOWN, WE ALL KNOW. WE KNOW WHAT FEELS GOOD AND WHAT DOESN'T.

Exercise: Tune out the noise

Write out which things you will intentionally tune out just for a period until you regain your coherence. What is the thing that is causing you to feel overwhelmed? Digital? Physical clutter? Obligations? Are people in your life creating noise? How do you simplify your schedule and your life? What is the first thing that comes to mind?

I say that we are in an endosymbiotic thermodynamic love affair with the sun. That's a very scientific way to say that we have to be sun lovers because we have evolved with it. If you want to heal, you have to start with getting your body into alignment with the sunlight.

CHAPTER 3

Crawl. Walk. Run:
You Are the Speed of Light

The Sun is the giver of life.

—Ramses II

If you drive by my house in the early morning, you will likely see me in my robe, sitting on my steps with a hot cup of coffee watching the sunrise. I live in Minnesota, but I will be there even when it's freezing. For as long as I can remember, I have had a love affair with the sun, especially the sunrise. There was always something about it that made me feel so alive, so hopeful. I always gaze at the sun in the morning and throughout the day, and I try to catch the last rays at sunset. I have become a full-blown sun worshiper; it is the key source of all of my health and happiness. That is entirely because of one person I met on this journey: Dr. Courtney Hunt.

Years ago, I stumbled upon Dr. Hunt's content on social media, where she discusses the relationship between quantum mechanics, the sun, and humans' ability to heal no matter how dire our chronic conditions may be. In fact, she believes that most of the dis-eases today are manifestations of a lack of interaction with the sun. What I absolutely loved about this woman was that she showed up every single day to teach live, she was a little spicy, and scientific data backed up her message. She has since amassed a huge social media following, continues to climb Camelback Mountain in Arizona every morning, and keeps creating content based on scientific research about the relationship between the sun, nutrition, and health. Although specific advice about physical health is beyond this book's scope, I do want to share some aspects of Dr. Hunt's research that have utterly changed my life and others' lives.

Dr. Hunt spent the majority of her medical career as a board-certified OB/GYN. In that capacity, she started noticing that increasingly more moms were chronically ill. Not feeling great herself, she committed to finding a solution and she set out on a journey of discovery. Diagnosed with Hashimoto's disease and hypothyroidism at age 35, the conditions caused weight gain, hair loss, and serious vaginal symptoms. Slowly but surely, she reversed the symptoms and weaned herself off all medication using the interventions she discovered in her research, which focused on information in three areas: light, mitochondria, and DNA.

Physical illness is often a sign of a deeper and more pervasive illness; we often ignore emotional and spiritual malaise and are taught to fix the physical symptoms of distress. My experience suggests that focusing on physical symptoms alone will not bring about the healing our bodies and minds truly need, and any form of healing is not limited to only the body or only the mind. Though I was called a "serial miscarrier" after losing nine pregnancies and I was told I would never carry a pregnancy to term, I

FOCUSING ON PHYSICAL SYMPTOMS ALONE WILL NOT BRING ABOUT THE HEALING OUR BODIES AND MINDS TRULY NEED

gave birth to two healthy children. I have healed my skin issues, ulcer pain, chronic PMS, headaches, tingling hands, heart palpitations, and so much more, not through Western medicine but through a changed lifestyle. Stories of physical healing are powerful in their own right, but what fascinates me most is our ability to heal *all* parts of ourselves by incorporating these practices. Dr. Hunt's experience bears this out as well: Not only did she heal her medical issues but also she vastly improved her cognitive abilities and emotional composition, and she is now able to study, learn, and share her research with others. Today she is committed to giving people the information they need to create the changes in their lifestyle that will help them on their journey to wellness.

First you crawl. Then walk. Then you run.

"How do we go outside when we are sick?" "I can't climb a mountain every day like you!" These are the types of response people often have when they first come into contact with Dr. Hunt. Her response is always: *First you crawl.* People hear these amazing stories of healing, and they want a way to fix everything all at once. It doesn't work that way. Author Marya Hornbacher wrote, "The desire for a quick or obvious fix is ridiculous. We found our way down here. Now we will find our way out."[17]

> "THE DESIRE FOR A QUICK OR OBVIOUS FIX IS RIDICULOUS. WE FOUND OUR WAY DOWN HERE. NOW WE WILL FIND OUR WAY OUT."

When you are seriously out of alignment, highly incoherent, unhappy, fragmented, and sick, the way out is always through, and we get through things by taking one step at a time. Often these are tiny steps; but we can still start with something, one thing, *anything*

---

17. Hornbacher, M. (2014). *Wasted: A Memoir of Bulimia and Anorexia* (updated edition). Harper Perennial.

that will get us out of inertia. Some courage and a whole lot of sheer will are involved. You crawl; you drag yourself out of your PJs and go outside. You can't do that? Then, you sit in your PJs on your porch and gaze at the sun while sipping hot coffee. You have to do something. Call someone, say something, do something. First you crawl.

Dr. Hunt grew up in Illinois. She knew she suffered from seasonal affective disorder and often wondered if she needed Prozac. She wasn't happy. The opportunity to study at UC Berkeley and then to do her residency at UCLA meant loads of sunshine; she noticed an immediate difference. When I speak to her, she tells me,

> As hard as residency was in California with some weeks doing over 100 hours a week, I felt happy. The whole time. I was happy. So, I knew it was the sun. And I knew that there was a feeling, even after a full night on call, delivering babies, that if I would drive east towards my house, I would feel better. So, I knew there was something there.

Then, as they say, life happened, bringing with it a busy career, marriage, small kids, no sleep, no sunshine, weight gain, anxiousness, and depression. As things went from bad to worse, Dr. Hunt did what many people do in this situation: she would have one or two glasses of wine every night to calm down. However, that affected her sleep and made everything worse. She says, "My brain was deteriorating, and I knew it was deteriorating. I was afraid I was going to have MS like my grandmother did, and I was also numb." She knew there had to be a better way.

She remembered her love of the sun and she started taking morning walks to soak it in; immediately, she noticed an improvement. However, she soon had a realization: her cognitive capacity was returning in force. She thought, "I can have thoughts about quantum field theory. I can have thoughts about computer software. I can have thoughts about medicine. I can have thoughts about bugs.

I can have thoughts about all this stuff and be integrated into one body of knowledge. I was retaining stuff again." Encouraged, she kept going, maintaining the changes she'd made in her physical routine, including much sunshine, exercise, and nutrition. Within a few years, she lost more than 30 pounds and no longer needed any medication. Her autoimmune condition disappeared. She was, by all accounts, a different person.[18]

Dr. Hunt tells me,

> I say that we are in an endosymbiotic thermodynamic love affair with the sun. That's a very scientific way to say that we have to be sun lovers because we have evolved with it. If you want to heal, you have to start with getting your body into alignment with the sunlight. It provides all of the instructions you need to start feeling better. The first step is to watch the sunrise every day. Start there. That light gives you all of the code you need to coordinate your mitochondria or batteries that make your energy. Sunrise and sunset alone will do a lot of good.

"WE ARE IN AN ENDO-SYMBIOTIC THERMO-DYNAMIC LOVE AFFAIR WITH THE SUN"

This advice can profoundly change your life. It has certainly made a huge difference in mine. It's so simple that it seems hard to believe that this single change could make our lives better. But it can.

---

18. Dr. Hunt stresses that she does sun exposure with ketosis, a metabolic state. Another important aspect of her process is fasting and autophagy: bodily function that flushes old or damaged cells and stimulates the regeneration of healthy cell renewal. This discovery won a Nobel Prize in physiology in 2016 and it's interesting to consider how every single religion teaches fasting. Hunt's book *Your Spark is Light* provides valuable data and personal insights about the process she's gone through.

"The sun has a huge spectrum of light, a field of electromagnetic radiation," Dr. Hunt continues. As the human body evolved, it did so according to the instructions, or code, provided by the full spectrum of sunlight; now, we only see 35 percent of that spectrum. Different aspects of the spectrum come through the atmosphere at different times of day, based on the angle of the sun in the sky. Dr. Hunt says, "These waves 'play' molecules in our body, in our eye, in our skin, like a magical symphony."

This is why we need the whole spectrum: it's code for our bodies to function properly. Unfortunately, most of us spend increasingly more time inside, without exposure to something that we simply cannot live without, the absence of which literally makes us sick. When we come into the sun, we cover our eyes with sunglasses and lather ourselves with sunscreen. The sun is our guide, our compass, and sort of a barometer. Dr Hunt equates the sun to our satellite that tells us if it's day or night, instructs the body whether to produce or shut off melatonin, which in turn, affects dopamine, serotonin, vitamin B, and a host of other physiological messengers in our body. Sunlight affects every single part of us as humans, and the effects of getting enough of it—or not—cascade through both our physical bodies and our lives.

No sun, no sleep

We spend as much as a third of our lives doing it. A third of each day is spent in this dormant state of body and mind. Even a few nights with very little sleep make us feel tired, agitated, and as if we've dulled (or entirely lost) our cognitive ability. This has happened to all of us on occasion. What's more common for a lot of people is getting less sleep than we need on a regular basis. Inadequate and poor-quality sleep are both linked with chronic diseases and conditions including type 2 diabetes, heart disease, obesity, and depression. Sleep affects every single system, organ, and aspect of our mind.

Research from Denmark[19] has shown that morning light relieves anxiety by reducing the activity of the brain's fear center. More broadly speaking, our exposure to light directly influences the quality of our sleep. Sleep deprivation is a common and perhaps deadly malady; and if we want to sleep well, sun exposure during the day is a must. The best way to improve sleep and balance melatonin is to get sun in your naked eyes at sunrise. When we sleep better, we balance our various functions and begin to feel better all around.

Reverse aging, but see yourself well

Dr. Hunt believes we have the ability to reverse the aging process ourselves. However, to do that, we have to see ourselves well. "In the world of quantum mechanics, time doesn't exist," she explains.

> The you 50 years from now is the you today. It's just how you collapse the wave function of your consciousness or how you decide to show up for the day.
>
> Understand that if you look in the mirror and see the person you want to be, you start letting go of the memories of who you were when you were sick. That will free you up to focus on changing things for your future. There are 86,400 seconds in the day. Each day you can take 10-15 of those seconds to change one thing. It might just be opening your window in the morning or rolling down your car window

"THERE ARE 86,400 SECONDS IN THE DAY. EACH DAY YOU CAN TAKE 10-15 OF THOSE SECONDS TO CHANGE ONE THING."

---

19. Sunlight Institute. (2023). *The sun & UV light.* https://sunlightinstitute.org/the-sun-and-uv-light/

when driving your kids to school, or arriving at your job five minutes earlier to sit in the parking lot to watch the sunrise. Your lifestyle is the symphony created by the quantum mechanics of your life.

Dr. Hunt notes that at the subatomic level, we—our thoughts, our actions, our bodies, and their effects—are composed of energy; and the way in which we direct (or misdirect) that energy has direct implications for us and for other people. She points out that in terms of quantum mechanics, everything we are and everything we do exists in the vast, interconnected energetic web called the Higgs field (which we'll get into further in Part III). Therefore, she says,

> Every time you wake up and you think, "I am a sad, upset, foggy person because of XYZ" or wonder, "Did my parents neglect me? Did my partner dump me? Was I bullied?" there is always a chance to start over. You leave your tracks on the universe, like a footprint in the sand in terms of the memories or the information you lay down. Every day you wake up and resort to memories that hold you down, every day you do the same negative thing over and over, is a day you can't get well. That's why mindfulness meditation works. That's why writing down goals and taping the information on your mirror works. So, use your 86,400 seconds of each day wisely and start to change every single tiny thing. Start with baby steps. Crawl, walk, run.

What's in one is in the whole, and as we heal our brains and bodies, we bring healing to our communities and to one another. "Heal one, heal all" is something I have heard Dr. Hunt say many times. When we are well, we affect others and the world. Our health isn't just a selfish desire to be better; it's a way to heal our families and communities, and to make an impact in the world. Dr. Hunt argues that the poor state of humanity's physical health is the primary cause of the global mental health crisis and even of sociocultural malaise. She contends that because our brains are inflamed, our mental health is off balance; we become sick and desperate, and we lash out. Being in the sun is the first step toward feeling better. Crawl. Walk. Run.

Exercise: Make time for the sun

Look at the sunrise every morning with naked eyes, even for a few minutes. It's that simple. Just gaze in the direction of the rising sun, even when cloudy or rainy. Repeat this twice more each day—two minutes looking toward the sun in the afternoon, and two minutes at sunset. If this is the only thing you do when it comes to the outdoors, this alone will change your mental and physical state.

Nature feeds my soul more than any human ever can. Nature is where I worship, where I feel I can be the true, imperfect me, without needing to prove, cajole, beg, or negotiate. It just gives of itself.

CHAPTER 4

The Trees Have Secrets to Tell You

Mother Nature's apothecary has a cure for almost every inner tur-moil of the soul. It's where the world, affairs and thoughts slow down, and we awake to the magic of being here and now. Sur-rounded by its beauty and without the noise of the world, we hear the silence of our soul that tells us everything will be ok. All is well.

—Anonymous

During my period of infertility, I was on a deep personal journey. Later, I began to realize that in some ways, that struggle allowed me to give birth to myself. At some point, there was a break in the clouds that allowed me to look up just long enough to ask, "What does this have to teach me?" By asking, I opened myself to the answers, which slowly started to emerge. I was being shown the path back to myself. It's almost as if that time was precisely the medicine I needed to heal; it allowed me to see things that were not aligned in my life. Books, people, and experiences appeared, each one a piece of the puzzle I was putting together without knowing what picture I was trying to create, what the result would ultimately be. Nature was one of those pieces.

One summer, in the wake of another miscarriage and another barrage of tests and pokes and bad news, my husband and I went to the Boundary Waters in Northern Minnesota. This was a trip that would forever leave a mark. We were looking for a hiking trail someone had recommended to us, and we got lost. In our search for the path that we'd meant to take, we came upon a beautiful little lake. Many things about it took our breath away—peaceful water, birdsong all around us, majestic trees surrounding the lake. We sat down, and for the next three hours, neither of us said a word. In that moment, with trees and silence surrounding us, I felt all heaviness leave me. As we sat there, I felt all the darkness in me release into the ground, and I started to feel my heart swell. I wasn't sad or filled with grief. I was happy. I was overcome with awe, the trees hugging me, almost as if they embraced me and gave me the deep sense of grounding I hadn't felt in years. I have always been a nature lover, but this was a truly holy experience. For the first time in a long time, I knew I was going to be okay. I knew I was going to be a mother one day. I don't know how I knew that, but I knew. My husband had a similar experience.

As we were leaving, we saw the name of the lake carved on a small wooden sign by the entrance, nearly covered with branches: Holy Lake.

The healing power of forest bathing

Trees are some of the oldest living organisms on the earth, and the oldest trees are the 4,600-year-old bristlecone pines. There is a part of us that simply comes into alignment and coherence when surrounded by nature, especially trees. This isn't just subjective: Research shows that we greatly benefit from being surrounded by trees, especially when we are in a forest or other tree-dense areas. The ancient practice that has arisen organically from humans' innate understanding of this benefit is *shinrin yoku*, a Japanese term that means *forest bathing*.

THERE IS A PART OF US THAT SIMPLY COMES INTO ALIGNMENT AND COHERENCE WHEN SURROUNDED BY NATURE

Introduced in the 1980s in Japan as a way to relieve stress and get more people to engage with nature, scientists quickly saw the effectiveness of the practice, observing numerous measurable changes in our bodies after just 20 minutes surrounded by trees.[20]

A brisk walk among the trees results in lower cortisol, the notorious stress hormone, as well as lowered blood pressure and an increase in natural killer cells—our immune system's main line of defense, which lower inflammation in the body, suppress cancer-causing cells and proteins, and much more. Those results were easily measured, but studies show there are a host of mental health and spiritual benefits as well: subjective measures still show a marked drop in anxiety, racing thoughts, anger, fatigue, and confusion.

This is a type of "medicine" to which most of us have free and ready access, and which, if we take it, can heal us on many levels and without side effects. All we have to do is go among the trees for 20 minutes.

What is it about the trees that creates such powerful benefits for the body, mind, and may I also add, soul?

We have evolved in nature and with nature. Our brain behaves differently in nature. The constant noise and overwhelmingness of human life and its many discontents slowly upset all of our systems, and we often don't notice until it's too late. Reconnecting with nature is resetting our brains. We cannot eliminate the ups and downs of

20. Harvard Medical School. (2019, July 1). A 20-minute nature break relieves stress. Harvard Health Publishing. https://www.health.harvard.edu/mind-and-mood/a-20-minute-nature-break-relieves-stress

**WE CANNOT ELIM-
INATE THE UPS AND
DOWNS OF LIFE, BUT
WE CAN FIND CALM
IN NATURE**

life, but we can find calm in nature. Yet, fewer and fewer of us are doing just that.

One of the best books I've read about the importance of nature for mental health is *Your Brain on Nature*, by Dr. Eva Selhub and Alan Logan.[21] This prescient book, published in 2014, anticipated the current crisis that is videophilia—the irresistible attraction of screens and inevitable impact on people: We have separated ourselves from nature, and it is profoundly damaging to our mental health.

In that same book, the authors write,

> Healers within various medical systems, from Ayurveda of the Indian subcontinent to traditional Chinese medicine, have long advocated nature exposure as a form of medicine. Within these healing systems, elements of nature—mountains, trees, plants, and bodies of water with the natural settings, are considered to be filled with an energy, a vital force that could be transferred to people in the promotion of health. As humans began to make a transition from rural life to urban civilizations, an even greater emphasis was placed on taking advantage of the medicinal effects of nature.

I've spoken to Dr. Selhub many times over the years about this topic. A pioneer of forest bathing in our country, her contribution to this conversation has been enormous. Yet, almost 10 years since the publication of this book, we find ourselves in even more dire circumstances. More than ever, we need to get out among the trees. It's free, it's accessible, and it's deeply healing for all of us.

---

21. Selhub, E., & Logan, A. (2014). *Your Brain on Nature*. Collins.

Exercise: Go hug a tree

At least once a week, practice forest bathing. (More if possible but start there.) While you are at it, go hug a tree: Go ahead, be the weirdo like me. Trust me, it will become second nature eventually.

Incredible trees

Trees produce something called phytoncides: organic compounds derived from plants that seem to have enormous benefits for the body. When it comes to protecting ourselves and strengthening our immune systems, the forest is our best friend. While extracting the compounds that come in the form of oils containing phytoncides and diffusing them indoors has some benefits, it is not nearly as powerful. So, what is it about the trees beyond the chemicals they secrete? Could it be the colors? Physical movement? Cleaner air? More oxygen in our bodies? It's certainly all these things; however, I believe there is so much more to this powerful medicine, something maybe not as easily measured by our current instruments, but something that we all undoubtedly feel. In his bestselling book *The Hidden Life of Trees*, Peter Wohlleben[22] writes about trees' innate adaptability, intelligence, and capacity to communicate with—and heal—other trees. We have evidence that they heal us as well.

In an interview with Yale School of the Environment, Wohlleben describes trees as, "highly sensitive and social beings… working together, they are cooperating with one another."[23] They do so by

---

22. Wohlleben, P. (2016). *The Hidden Life of Trees: What They Feel, How They Communicate*. Greystone Books.
23. Schiffman, R. (2016, November 16). Are trees sentient beings? Certainly, says German forester. *YaleEnvironment360*. https://e360.yale.edu/features/are_trees_sentient_peter_wohlleben

feeding sick trees outside of their species through their incredibly complex root system. Trees talk to each other, offering nourishment and protection. Wohlleben proposes that trees may even have consciousness, a theory supported by David Hawkins's Map of Consciousness[24], a tool developed to explore the connections between consciousness and our emotional positionality in the world.

If trees are sentient and conscious, they know that we are there. If they have an extensive underground network that allows them to communicate with each other, we can tap into that network as well and it can support us. Furthermore, if we recognize the implications of quantum mechanics, particularly its assertion that all things are connected through the Higgs field, we begin to grasp the depth to which this interconnectedness goes—and that we are an integral part of this vast quantum web. When we pause long enough to encounter the forest's wordless power, we tap into our capacity for wonder and awe and we activate our healing potential in ways we may always be able to explain but cannot really deny. Trees have secrets to tell us; we need only listen.

Nature equals abundance

Years ago, my business was extremely busy, and with two small children at home, I felt like I never had the time I needed to be in the woods. A walk in the forest seemed like a waste of time, a wasted opportunity to bring in money or grow my business. So, I deliberately turned this around by telling myself that by walking in the woods, I was making more money. I know this sounds like positive mumbo-jumbo that could never possibly work, but this one shift in perspective profoundly changed my life.

---

24. Hawkins, D. (2020). *The Map of Consciousness Explained: A Proven Energy Scale to Actualize Your Ultimate Potential*. Hay House Inc.

Intention changes physical matter, as we'll explore further in Part II. By shifting my intention, I began to reinforce this belief that every time I took a walk in the middle of the day, I was making more money. By doing something I profoundly enjoyed and putting myself in a state of ease, I gave myself the break I desperately needed, and I created a mental correlation (a quantum bridge, which we'll explore) between the ease I found in nature and the success I wanted to achieve. Because I was more relaxed, healthier, and happier, I was more present and productive at work. I had the most incredible ideas and guidance while in the forest, and my business continued to grow—not *despite* that I was taking the time out of my day to go for a walk in the forest, but *because* I was.

It seems an overreach to say, but it's true: Nature will give you whatever you need. Why? Getting out-

NATURE WILL GIVE YOU WHATEVER YOU NEED

side forces you to step out of your self-created cage of thoughts and limitations and it opens you up to what is. It opens you up to possibility. It opens you up to a physical, mental, and spiritual exhale, a powerful, cathartic, and necessary release. I like to think that nature takes all my emotional chaos and transforms it into something clear; like alchemy, nature takes the dross of my thoughts and purifies them, turning them into gold. Nature feeds my soul more than any human ever can. Nature is where I worship, where I feel I can be the true, imperfect me, without needing to prove, cajole, beg, or negotiate. It just gives of itself.

Research has long shown that walking in nature lowers anxiety, depression, anger, fatigue, and confusion.[25] It calms a racing mind and reduces the feeling of overwhelm. It doesn't cost a thing. It welcomes us with open arms. We just have to show up.

---

25. Li, Q. et al. (2022). Effects of forest bathing (shinrin-yoku) on serotonin in serum, depressive symptoms and subjective sleep quality in middle-aged males. *Environmental Health and Preventative Medicine, 27*(44). doi: 10.1265/ehpm.22-00136

Jaime Taets, founder of Keystone Group International, gets answers from going outdoors, whether hiking, walking, or running. She says,

> I start every run with an issue or a thing that I am anxious about, and I put it out there at the start of my run and just kind of work through it as I'm running. And the ideas come to me, and my subconscious comes forward. That is the spiritual piece. It's allowing my subconscious to solve the problems because I believe thoroughly that the answers to my problems are already there. I've got too much of a monkey brain every day, all day, because of everything that's going on that I don't allow it to come forward. And I started to get really curious about what is actually happening, why is this happening only while running? I think it's because I am open to it, and a place where I can hear the guidance. Instead of being so distracted with everything else, I am creating space for it.

So, even if you find it difficult to relinquish the things you are grasping onto because of societal expectations or an addiction to technology, maybe adding a walk in the woods is what the doctor ordered. If we can take that small step, we can move into a more relaxed and peaceful state of mind, slowing the pace of our lives. Soon, we may find ourselves making different choices, shifting our priorities, and setting different goals.

SLOW DOWN THE CHATTER AND LISTEN TO THE WHISPERS OF YOUR OWN SOUL

Just go outside. State an intention of letting go of whatever is weighing on your heart; ask for resolution or guidance, and just go outside. Go for 10 minutes. Fall in love with what the outdoors has to offer. Slow down the chatter and listen to the whispers of your own soul. You do know what to do. You can do that. You *do* have the answers, but you have to listen.

Nature doesn't force, doesn't yell, and doesn't impose. It is my favorite place to be. It's where the world and my thoughts slow down, and I awaken to the magic of being in the here and now. The majesty of natural surroundings always gives me more than I could ever ask for. Now more than ever, it's imperative we connect with this powerful force and absorb the health and beauty that abounds there. May it give you everything you want and need.

What does one do in cold winters or hot summers, when there are no leaves on the trees, or when the weather is too harsh to go outside? Nature is always alive and ready to embrace us regardless of what it looks like. The physical, mental, emotional, and spiritual benefits are still available to us, and we can creatively use this research to reap the benefits. Even in Minnesota, where I've lived for over 20 years, we can still go out even for a few minutes. It's sort of micro-dosing, just enough to come into contact with nature and receive a breath of fresh air. As I write this, it is December: snow covers the ground, the sidewalks and streets, and it is *cold*. However, the sun was out, so I bundled up and took a break. My intention was to go out for just 15 minutes, but I walked for nearly an hour—it just felt so invigorating to be outside. Most of the time, it's not the cold we have to fight; it's inertia, and our thoughts telling us to choose the comfort of sameness, the warm living room in winter or the relaxing air conditioning in summer, over the movement and direct contact with sunlight, air, and trees that our bodies and minds desperately need.

We can also feed these needs by providing the mind and body with the stimuli found in nature through imagery, smells, and sounds, like recordings of moving water, birds, or rain coupled with candles or essential oils. In fact, the essential oils from cypress trees have been proven to promote relaxation and boost immunity. Having plants around us—even fake plants!—completely reshapes our relationship to the spaces we're in and our feeling and thought states when we're in them, so we can "condition" our indoor spaces with life force and vitality.

Henry David Thoreau wrote,

There is nothing so sanative, so poetic, as a walk in the woods and fields even now, when I meet none abroad for pleasure. In the street and in society I am almost invariably cheap and dissipated, my life is unspeakably mean. No amount of gold or respectability would in the least redeem it—dining with the Governor or a member of Congress!! But alone in distant woods or fields, I come to myself, I once more feel myself grandly related, and that cold and solitude are friends of mine. I suppose that this value, in my case, is equivalent to what others get by churchgoing and prayer. I thus dispose of the superfluous and see things as they are, grand and beautiful.[26]

"ALONE IN DISTANT WOODS OR FIELDS, I COME TO MYSELF"

---

26. Thoreau, H. D. (2009). *The Journal of Henry David Thoreau, 1837–1861*. New York Review Books Classics.

Exercise: Practice forest bathing

Enter a forest or an area with many trees. As you start walking, be reminded of your life force: the breath. A deep inhale and exhale can be a remedy for many life's ills. Walk slowly and deliberately, focusing on your senses and what they receive from their natural surroundings: the smell of the trees and the earth, the texture of the bark and leaves. Allow yourself to explore the connection that has existed since the beginning of time. Engage all of your senses and let go of the social world, just for this moment in time, knowing with certainty that you will receive what you need. Hug a tree. Close your eyes and see if you can sense the surge of energy and life force that can come from such an encounter. Yes, you will look weird to yourself and others but, just like lovers once separated and then reunited, soon enough, it simply won't matter what anyone thinks.

Here are the steps I take when I need spiritual guidance, which I reliably receive in my forest-bathing practice.

1. State your intention. A clear, focused intention can bring you to the answers and help you when you are in need.
2. Hug a tree. Close your eyes with your hands on the tree and sense the force of energy it generates. Allow that energy to be transferred into you.
3. Touch the trees; feel their leaves, bark, branches, and flowers.
4. Ask a question, something with which you have been struggling.
5. Ask the trees to help you release it—the question or struggle—and let it go.
6. Give thanks for what trees do for us.
7. Trust that it has been handled.

A resonant moment is one in which you feel like your entire being is in sync with the universe. Everything feels right, in its place, like things have somehow come together, and you're exactly where you need to be. You sense that you're on the right path; everything before has conspired to bring you to this point. It's the feeling of being fully alive, present, and deeply connected. You feel your oneness with the universe.

CHAPTER 5

Increase Your Vibe and Energy: Resonance

If you want to know the secrets of the universe, think in terms of energy, frequency, and vibrations.

—Nikola Tesla, Serbian-American
engineer, physicist, and futurist

A few years ago, I was sitting on the couch with my kids on my lap for our regular morning cuddles. I'd just finished my daily meditations and writing, and contemplative music played softly. I was stroking their hair, their faces filled with morning sun; they were silent and content, as was I. In a flash, I thought of the painful time in my life when I was struggling with miscarriages and a deep longing for children. Then I was overcome with gratitude for the moment I was in: the cuddles, my healthy children and harmonious

A RESONANT MOMENT IS ONE IN WHICH YOU FEEL LIKE YOUR ENTIRE BEING IS IN SYNC WITH THE UNIVERSE family, the sunshine and warmth, the music, the safety, my life's purpose, and my peace of mind. It was a moment I will remember and cherish forever, one of alignment, coherence, and resonance.

A resonant moment is one in which you feel like your entire being is in sync with the universe. Everything feels right, in its place, like things have somehow come together, and you're exactly where you need to be. You sense that you're on the right path; everything before has conspired to bring you to this point. It's the feeling of being fully alive, present, and deeply connected. You feel your oneness with the universe.

These moments are not random, but rather the result of our inner and outer experience coming into alignment. When we feel good about what is happening within ourselves, external circumstances seem to fall into place around us as well. We can create these moments by focusing on the things that matter most and letting go of those things which do not serve our highest good. The more we focus on things that are important to us, the more our lives will be filled with these moments. We can create resonance within ourselves through the easy and accessible ways I will describe.

The majority of our lives should be spent in resonant moments. This is what mystics have referred to when saying that miracles are a daily occurrence and an expectation, should we actually pay attention to see. However, the many variables of life—the baggage and heaviness and responsibilities, the other people, the moving parts— can take us out of resonance, stealing our sense of connection, presence, and focus. When we spend too long away from our connection to what makes us feel aligned, we may forget how to return.

Frequency. Vibration. Resonance. All these terms are creeping into common parlance, but what do they mean? Is it actually possible to change our energy? How? We may dismiss these concepts because they are often linked to equally nebulous terms such as "source" and "universe." In truth, you don't have to buy into woo-woo mumbo-jumbo to understand these principles and incorporate their implications to benefit your life.

All matter is made of particles, dark matter included, which is the majority of our universe. When not observed, these particles are actually waves; they are energy in a state of

> **WHEN NOT OBSERVED, THESE PARTICLES ARE ACTUALLY WAVES; THEY ARE ENERGY IN A STATE OF CONSTANT VIBRATION**

constant vibration. They are "held" together by the Higgs field, the energetic force that connects everything and everyone. We are part of that field.

Late in his career, as quantum physics advanced, significantly reshaping our understanding of the nature of the physical world, Albert Einstein wrote, "Concerning matter, we have been all wrong. What we have called matter is energy, whose vibration has been so lowered as to be perceptible to the senses. There is no matter."

The first law of thermodynamics states that energy cannot be created or destroyed. However, it can be transferred from one location to another and converted to and from other energy forms. Energy can be molded; its form, function, and purpose—and ours—can be changed.

In Gloria Perma's book, physicist Max Planck put it plainly:

All the physical matters are composed of vibration. As a man who has devoted his whole life to the most clear-headed science, to the study of matter, I can tell you as a result of my research about atoms this much: There is no matter as such. All matter originates and exists only by virtue of a force, which brings the particle of an atom to vibration and holds this most minute solar system of the atom together. We must assume behind this force the existence of a conscious and intelligent mind. This mind is the matrix of all matter.[27]

In short, everything in the universe is made up of particles vibrating at different speeds—trees and water and rocks; our bodies, emotions, and thoughts. Some particles vibrate at higher speeds, some at lower. Lower vibrations feel dense, heavy, and stagnant. Higher vibrations feel lighter. Emotions such as sadness and anger vibrate lower than emotions such as love and joy.

We ourselves are vibrating waves of energy, slowed down to the point at which we are perceived as matter. That matter—us, at the subatomic level—is still in motion; a wide range of things can excite our energy to higher vibrations, such as heat and cold, music and emotion. We emanate energy, and we perceive others' energy as

WE EMANATE ENERGY, AND WE PERCEIVE OTHERS' ENERGY AS WELL

well; we might sense that we do (or don't) like a person's "vibe." We feel others' vibration, just as they feel and are influenced by ours. Our emotions influence the energy we emanate; the majority of our energetic vibration comes from the heart. That's where resonance comes in.

At a strictly scientific level, resonance is the phenomenon that occurs when two similar systems influence each other and begin to vibrate at the same frequency. When this happens, the two systems interact with one another through a series of positive feedback loops that intensify and amplify over time. Resonance occurs when a vibration or sound matches another vibration or sound.

No wonder we use the word "resonant" to describe moments that feel harmonious and in tune. At the level of human experience, when something resonates with you, it means it has a similar note or feeling as your energy. So, when you experience resonance in life, it's like

---

27. Prema, G. (2022). *It's All Light: Juicy Science Meets Spirituality Without Religion*, p. 78. Independently Published

hearing your song played back at you—you know exactly how someone feels because it's how you feel too. Resonance can be thought of as the "frequency" or vibration at which you operate in life.

I spoke to Gloria Prema, author of *It's All Light*, about resonance, and here's what she said.

> **"WHEN YOU WANT TO ATTRACT SOMETHING, YOU REALLY HAVE TO BE IN THE SAME RESONANCE AS IT"**

When you want to attract something, you really have to be in the same resonance as it. The law of attraction—I think it's a slight misnomer. I think it should be the law of resonance. There are various experiments that will demonstrate this; for example, there's one that showed that when you put pendulum clocks in a room together, the one with the strongest resonance will set all the others off in the same rhythm. Same with guitar strings. If you have several guitars in the room and the A string [is played], all the A strings of the other guitars will start to vibrate because of sympathetic resonance. It's the law of nature. And I think what [has] slightly misled people about the law of attraction [is] not understanding that you have to be in the resonance of what you want to attract or what you want to have.

The law of attraction is really a law of resonance

Dr. Nisha Manek expands on the distinction between attraction and resonance by saying that the concept of the law of attraction was "a good starting point" for people to begin thinking about how their states of consciousness influence the outcomes in their lives. She compares consciousness to a magnetic field: it draws things toward itself. Inside the field, iron filings—you—are attracted. It is not so much that the past pushes us toward a certain future, but that when we are rooted in the past, we attract outcomes similar to those we've already had and to what is familiar. However, as we detach from past perceptions and deepen our understanding of future potential, we become more available to something beyond just attraction—in other words, we become available to real resonance.

"You're becoming," Manek says. "You have divine help, and ultimately, you are also divine. You have to reach that divinity within yourself, manifest by becoming that. Not attracting. You *are* that."

The law of resonance describes the degree to which we vibrate with the thing we desire. Are we on the same wavelength or are we clashing? Resonance is a deep knowing that we are worthy of and aligned with our desires. It's the absence of doubt and of limiting beliefs, which clash with the energy of what we want to attract.

We all want different things in life, and we work hard to get those things; but they are often elusive, and many people remain in a state of constant striving and become frustrated. This frustration leads to unhappiness and much of our suffering. When we are frustrated, we tend to blame ourselves for not being good enough or we blame others for not giving us what we want.

By focusing solely on not having what we want—on what we lack—we emphasize its absence; we remain out of resonance with it, and it remains out of reach. The goal, then, is to get into resonance with it. We do that through words and actions, not wishful thinking.

What and who you consume

Our mental diet affects our resonance. This includes the music we listen to, the books we read, and yes, the news and entertainment we consume. Gloria Prema explains the influence of this input on our energetic states, including the vibration we create.

Every particle both rotates and vibrates up and down. We have this frequency going on all the time. Resonance is just what we are vibrating to. Our body, our thoughts, our emotions, all of it has a particular frequency, and that's our resonance, but it can be shifted. I use the analogy of a radio or a TV set. If you want to change your frequency, you turn the dial. If you're watching television, you have a picture, you have a sound. Well, if you turn the dial, you pick up a different frequency, you have a completely different picture, a completely different sound. It's the same thing with us; it's a case of tuning to a different frequency. And another way to do that is through meditation. That's a powerful way to change your frequency.

We are all energy antennae

Being around other people is a way of changing our resonance. This serves as a powerful reminder to be mindful about where and with whom we spend our time. If we are in the same resonance as the people around us, we will pick up on similar thoughts and habits. When we're surrounded with negative and self-absorbed people, that energy will affect us; the people with whom we surround ourselves play a vital role in our ability to heal.

Our environment matters because it carries information, it carries energy. Because we are energy antennas, we pick up the frequency of everything and everyone in our sphere. Energy vampires are real, but so are sunshine people—those who are always a joy to be around. Whatever we do, wherever we spend our time, whatever company we keep, if we stay in connection with it long enough, it leaves an imprint on us.

OUR ENVIRONMENT MATTERS BECAUSE IT CARRIES INFORMATION, IT CARRIES ENERGY

89

Many of us felt this during pandemic shutdowns, when we didn't have to be around people we didn't want to see. When I talked to Minneapolis-based entrepreneur Hayley Matthews-Jones, she said this provided a powerful lesson for her, and has led to a permanent shift in what guides the way she spends her time.

> Go where you have a conversation with someone, and you come away from it feeling motivated and inspired and excited and full of love and passion. That is the energy you should chase. That's the thing that I'm trying to cultivate—listening to that gut instinct. And that's not to say that you'll never do anything you don't enjoy but follow your true values and your true energy. I think a lot of people get distracted [from that], especially younger people.

Sometimes we just don't have the confidence to say, "I don't feel good around this person." It takes a while to learn to listen to that inner nudge, let alone to trust it. That comes bit by bit. Often, our body will tell us things our brain is not yet ready to hear. You start to heed the instinct that tells you not to engage with that person, or says simply, "Leave now." The more you listen to these inner cues, the more confident you will become in their wisdom.

This takes on even more importance when we start to think in terms of resonance and energy transfer. Gloria Prema is clear about the influence of the people in our lives who can cause us to raise or lose resonance. She says,

> They say that there are five people we spend most of our lives with. Those are the ones who we end up becoming like, because we're in the same resonance. We adopt the same habits, the same thoughts, same frequencies. If you're not happy where you are, look for mentors, people who have the energy, the resonance of what you want to be or who you want to become,

and hang around them. Befriend them or follow them online.

> **"LOOK FOR MENTORS, PEOPLE WHO HAVE THE ENERGY, THE RESONANCE OF WHAT YOU WANT TO BE OR WHO YOU WANT TO BECOME"**

Just as there are things that can make us feel better, there are things that can negatively affect our vibe. Dr. John Diamond, in his book *Your Body Doesn't Lie*,[28] used kinesiology and muscle testing to prove the correlation between negative images and situations and our emotional and energetic state. He found that when we have negative emotions such as anger, frustration, and resentment, our energy field becomes distorted. This can be measured by muscle testing your arm strength before and after a picture intervention. That is, Diamond found that when people were shown negative images, their muscle strength was reduced by up to half. He also found that when people were shown positive images, their strength *increased* by up to half. This suggests that what we see, hear, and feel directly affects our energy field. So, we need to be very careful about what we allow into our field.

This takes us back to the importance of tuning out the noise and limiting the inputs that weaken us, create incoherence, and affect our vibration. This is also why looking at even images of nature, smiling children, or overall positive images strengthens us. It is why it's important to condition our homes and our minds with beautiful, uplifting, and inspiring elements.

In *Power vs. Force: The Hidden Determinants of Human Behavior*, Dr. David Hawkins[29] explains there are 10 levels of consciousness, each representing a different level of awareness and experience in life—from the most primitive level (0-39) all the way up to enlightenment (1,000).

---

28. Diamond, J. (1980). *Your Body Doesn't Lie*. Warner Books.
29. Hawkins, D. (2014). *Power vs. Force: The Hidden Determinants of Human Behavior*. Hay House Inc.

Hawkins, a psychiatrist, underwent several life-changing experiences that led to dramatic shifts in his consciousness. He noticed that his level of consciousness was no longer based on ego or mind but on a state of overwhelming joy and was powerfully connected to the "presence"—a blissful state that helped him develop a map of consciousness. This map shows the different levels of human consciousness and associated energy fields. It also shows the mutual influence of each level of consciousness on our thoughts and feelings and vice versa. Dawkins identifies nine levels of consciousness. The lowest level is fear based and operates in survival mode while the highest level is love based and operates from a place of inner peace and joy. So, when we are in a state of fear, we are operating from a lower level of consciousness, and this is reflected in our thoughts, feelings, and actions.

The map also shows how emotions affect our energetic vibration. The higher our vibration, the happier we are—and the more successful we are in life. In contrast, if our vibration is low, it will be easy for us to feel negative emotions such as anger or fear, which can make it hard for us to succeed in any area of our lives: business, relationships, or health.

When we move up the levels of consciousness to love-based or higher levels, our thoughts become more positive in nature, we feel happier and there is an increase in energy flow, like a current of electricity that flows through our bodies. When we are in fear-based consciousness, that flow of energy is blocked; we feel tired and drained. As we rise through states of consciousness, these blocks are removed, and more energy can flow through us. This increase in energy also has an effect on how we manifest things into our lives—there is an increase in synchronicity and coincidence as well as better overall health and wellbeing.

Exercise: Who you surround yourself with inventory

Make an inventory of people with whom you surround yourself. Who are the people that make you feel great? Who fits into the energy vampire category? Be honest with yourself. Make a conscious effort to surround yourself with those people who are good for you and help raise your resonance.

A note about animals and resonance

Animals are often such great companions and they can help us be more resonant because of their own "in the present moment" resonance. They can also feel our resonance. They might even feel energy more readily than we do because they have to rely on it more. Near my hometown in Bosnia, there is a herd of wild horses that move from pasture to pasture. Photographers love taking photographs of them and trying to get close to them—not everyone succeeds. Last year, on a cold spring day, my brother headed out to see them. He spent a significant amount of time just watching them at a distance, appreciating the beauty and getting himself into alignment and high resonance. Then, he approached them and spent an hour in their midst at sunset and captured the most breathtaking photos that you can see on my website.[30] These images hang in my office as a reminder of resonant moments and the beauty that surrounds us.

Expanded heart field

The HeartMath Institute[31] is a leader in heart coherence research. They describe heart coherence as a field emanating from and surrounding the human body. The electromagnetic field of the heart

---

30. www.jasnaburza.com/healerinheels
31. HeartMath Institute. (n.d.). *HeartMath Institute.* https://www.heartmath.org/

"THE HEART IS REALLY THE POWER ORGAN OF THE BODY." is 5,000 times stronger than that of the brain. As Gloria Prema says, "The heart is really the power organ of the body." I believe that most of us can feel this, but maybe, like intuition, we have learned to ignore it while giving more attention to our logical minds.

Heart coherence puts us in a state of greater resonance. Research from the HeartMath[32] Institute indicates that, "One's ability to self-regulate the quality of feeling and emotion of one's moment-to-moment experience influences our physiology and the reciprocal interactions between physiological, cognitive, and emotional systems. Self-induced positive emotion is reflected in the pattern of one's heart's rhythm, which in turn increases the coherence in bodily processes."

The HeartMath Institute's research on the patterns and rhythms various physiological systems generate during the experience of different emotions shows that sustained positive emotions associate with a noticeably coherent, smooth, and balanced heart-rhythm pattern. In contrast, negative emotions are reflected by a jagged, erratic pattern. This is consistent with what is known about resonance and has major implications for our daily lives.

Thoughts and feelings are energies that operate on different vibrations. The vibration is determined by the quality of our thoughts, feelings, attitudes and behaviors throughout the day. Higher thoughts and feelings add an uplifting tone through our day. In our higher thought vibrations, we're more caring, compassionate and kind with each other. We feel more self-secure and resilient in life's interactions. Lower vibrational thoughts and feelings bring us down. This results in unhappiness and feelings of separation from others

---

32. HeartMath Institute. (n.d.). *The science of coherence: Why does coherence matter?* https://www.heartmath.org/heart-coherence/science/

due to judgments or blame. We worry more, experience low self-security and can be too hard on ourselves and others.[33]

Redirecting strong negative emotions is not easy and it takes time, but it is doable. We start climbing down the ladder of negative charge or behavior, step by step. However, getting into heart coherence is one of the fastest ways to do that. As Gloria Prema points out, "Coherence is a harmonious state where our hearts, minds and bodies are united in cooperation and flow."

She continues,

I think that's probably the reason why all the [spiritual] teachers have taught us to love one another. Align with love. Whatever tradition you feel you resonate most with, as long as it's love. What the world needs now is love. It is the most powerful thing. But I would say that you should never prescribe to someone, you must do it this way, you must do it that way, because then you're in the realm of religion. I completely understand why people want to follow religion. I have no problem with that. But honestly, the only caveat is that it's love. Are you learning love? Are you learning *to* love? That's the only thing I would say. As long as you can connect with love yourself, you'll be okay.

> **"THE ONLY CAVEAT IS THAT IT'S LOVE. ARE YOU LEARNING LOVE? ARE YOU LEARNING *TO* LOVE?"**

---

33. HeartMath. (n.d.). *Raising our vibration to access our higher potentials.* https://www.heartmath.com/add_heart_call/raising-our-vibration-to-access-our-higher-potentials/

How to change your resonance and increase your vibration

Yes, life happens, and yes, we are influenced by our environment. However, we also have the power to protect our energy and create resonant moments. When outside factors interfere and overpower us, we can still use these techniques to return to our coherence and regain a high vibrational state.

The following activities and aspects are just a few things that have been proven to change our physiological and mental state, raising our vibration and restoring our ability to resonate with what we desire. All we have to do is find out which techniques work for us. Just as a child must find ways to self-soothe, so must we.

Recontextualization, redux

We are all capable of changing our emotional state by changing our thoughts. The most important thing to note is that emotions are not facts; they are responses to our interpretation of events. This means that you can choose how you feel at any moment simply by changing the way you interpret what is happening around you. While this may sound like a lot of work, it's actually pretty easy. Most people don't realize they are constantly interpreting what is happening around them. For example, let's say your boss tells you he needs you to complete a report by the end of the day. Some people would interpret that statement to mean that their boss is angry with them or that they've done something wrong. What if instead of interpreting his statement as an attack on your character, you interpreted it as a request for help? What if you thought about it as a way for him to get what he needed, instead of thinking that he was upset with you? By changing the way in which you interpret what is happening around you, you can change your feelings about any situation and your response.

Physical activity

Physical movement creates an immediate change in emotional state. If we want to feel more confident and powerful, we can do so by engaging in physical activity that makes us feel like a superhero (or at least releases endorphins and makes us feel strong). If we're under stress, we can stretch, walk, or go for a run. If we have anxiety about something in our lives, we can try dancing it away! Physical activity lifts our mood and makes us feel more in control of our lives.

Enclothed cognition

My husband and friends laugh when I say this, but when I wear a wide-brimmed hat, big earrings, and good heels, I immediately feel different. I feel confident, healthy, energetic, and at ease. It truly feels like coming home; it's comfort. Likewise, when I'm in leggings and tennis shoes, I feel ready to move my body. The simple change of clothes also changes my mindset, allowing me to embody literally the person I need to be for the task ahead.

What we wear can shift how we feel in a significant way. By wearing a certain shirt or tie, we can feel more confident and powerful. We can also

> **WHAT WE WEAR CAN SHIFT HOW WE FEEL IN A SIGNIFICANT WAY**

reduce our confidence by wearing something that makes us feel uncomfortable or ill at ease. The mental shift is called "enclothed cognition," and its effects are measurable. In one experiment[34] researchers asked subjects to perform a task while wearing a white lab coat or a black one. The white coat made people more productive (even

---

34. Hajo, A., & Galinksy, A. (2012). Enclothed cognition. *Journal of Experimental Social Psychology, 48*(4), 918-925.

though it was identical in every other way). In another study[35] subjects who wore a doctor's stethoscope performed better on memory tests than those who didn't wear one. Clothes have the power to change our emotional state and therefore our behavior.

Meditation

I started dabbling with meditation when I was in college. I knew the benefits, but I just couldn't figure it out. My mind wandered incessantly; I just didn't have the patience to do it. Gradually, I found my meditation niche in the affirmations of Stin Hansen (her podcast "My Thought Coach" has been a dear friend for over 15 years).[36] Affirmations have helped me train my mind, teaching me to be still for a few more minutes every time.

I know that when I meditate, I feel better; my energy is clearer and more peaceful, and I have a more aligned day. My perspective on life changes for the better. My worries and fears diminish. My heart opens more to love. I still forget to do it—life happens—but the moment I feel out of alignment and recognize that I have lost coherence, I know it is time to meditate again. It heightens my vibration and restores my peace.

Music

I woke up this morning feeling restless. The last few days I have not been intentional about my spirituality and journaling, both of which help me stay centered and creative. I turned on my "spiritual

---

35. Blakeslee, S. (2012, April 2). Mind games: Sometimes a white coat isn't just a white coat. *The New York Times*. https://www.nytimes.com/2012/04/03/science/clothes-and-self-perception.html

36. Hansen, S. (n.d.). My thought coach. https://www.mythoughtcoach.com/

mornings playlist" and heard a beautiful Gaelic prayer set to music, creating an immediate sense of resonance, and reminding me to pick up my pen and write. This is a playlist I've had playing while I've written in the past; now my brain is conditioned to connect these positive factors, to identify alignment and resonance even in small details. These connections can be strengthened in every area of our lives: exercise, time with kids, writing, spirituality, sensuality. You know that feeling when your song plays? When you are dancing with others? It's electric. You feel the energy in the room and that energy affects you. That's the power of resonance and vibration; that's the power of matching energy. Music primes our ability to feel resonance, evoking the emotions and thoughts we need when we feel restless or stuck. Create a playlist for any activity; the music will become a conditioning tool that can help you change your state at any time.

> **MUSIC PRIMES OUR ABILITY TO FEEL RESONANCE**

Expand your heart field

This is an exercise I learned from the HeartMath Institute: Find a comfortable place to sit and slow down your breath by taking a few deep inhales and few deep exhales. Then, focus your attention in your heart area, maybe even place your hands on your chest. Think of something or someone you appreciate deeply. Let this emotion permeate your being. I like to think of someone I love very much and smile as I think of them. Stay in this space for a few moments. Research is conclusive on the benefits of doing this. I suggest visiting the HeartMath Institute website to get access to many more wonderful tools.

When nothing goes right

So, what do we do when we wake up annoyed, frustrated, short with ourselves and others—in other words, when we're turning into a tornado of emotion that's going to disturb everyone in our way?

You know that's not who you really are. It's only when external and internal stressors of life overwhelm us past our capacity that we lose our footing. That looks different for everyone. Some will self-medicate through food or wine, some lose their temper, some withdraw from the world and take shelter in silence. We all become some other person we don't like when we're triggered and unable to process what's going on. Self-awareness can help us identify those triggers and get better at skillfully deescalating ourselves.

This process requires humility—a hard thing to come by in a world that tells us we always have to be (or at least seem to be) right. However, if we can catch ourselves in that moment, we can change our vibration and check the incoherent energy we're about to spill into the day. Just like airplanes have a destination, we can constantly course correct to stay on our path.

We're often far more disciplined about our diet, fitness, or professional obligations than we are about our vibration and the energy we put into the world. So if you find yourself in the middle of a crappy day and sense that you're sending out a bad vibe, slow down. Let that negative energy fizzle out. Find your way back to neutral. We can't go from 300 mph to zero by slamming the brakes; we'll spin out of control, or just (literally) flip. Let the emotions flow through, acknowledging them as they leave. These moments are to be expected, not resisted.

> WE CAN'T GO FROM 300 MPH TO ZERO BY SLAMMING THE BRAKES

Take a nap, go for a walk, spend some time alone. This often isn't the time to be creative or productive. Allow yourself to reset, releasing the chaotic energy and allowing yourself to resonate, once again, with harmony and peace.

Exercise: The 'change your vibration' challenge

Besides all the practices I have already mentioned in this chapter, here is a list of practical ways we can all change our "vibe" relatively quickly.

1. **Do something nice for others.** Offer a kind word, let someone cut in front of you in a line, go get coffee for a coworker. Adding positive energy to others' lives will raise their vibration as well as your own.
2. **Pay it forward.** You've heard of people paying for coffee or parking for the person behind them. Do it. Start a movement or a trend that would not only make someone's day but encourage them to do the same.
3. **Do something unexpected.** Take a ballet class, go salsa dancing, or stay home with popcorn and a movie if you typically like to go out.
4. **Unplug.** Find at least 10 minutes to just sit in silence. Close your eyes and breathe in and out.

PART II

THE OBSERVER EFFECT AND THE POWER OF INTENTION

Once we have slowed down things enough to shift from chaos to coherence (we constantly fall in and out of coherence, so our practices to sustain it must be ongoing, like daily showers), then we can consciously and with intention become creators of our own reality. Quantum physics and the study of intention can show us how to do just that.

In the simplest terms, what you focus on becomes your reality. In the realm of quantum physics, there is something called the **observer effect** that explains how human observation changes the behavior of particles.

The observer effect is the phenomenon in which the act of observation alters the behavior of the particles being observed. This effect is due to the wave-like nature of matter, which means that particles can exist in multiple states simultaneously. When an observer measures a particular property of a particle, they are effectively collapsing the wave-function of that particle, causing it to assume a definite state.[37]

Another way to think about this is even simpler: Basically, what you see and place attention on is what you get.

For example, if you are flipping through channels on your TV, all of those programs are available to you simultaneously. However, the only one that will make it into your reality is the one you watch. The ones you are not watching are still out there, but you are choosing to focus on the one in front of you. Our reality is much the same: At any given moment, there is a huge array of channels playing out as potentialities in the Higgs field, which will be explored more fully in Part III. For now, the critical thing to know is that there are a vast number of possible experiences available to you in the field of your imagination. The nature of your experiences and the trajectory of your life are determined by many different factors, over which you may or may not have control; but there is no question that one of those factors, maybe the most powerful, is your very own "observer effect."

Do me a favor. Close your eyes and call up two images on the screen of your mind: you happy and smiling, and you frowning and upset. Even now, you are projecting potential scenarios, or potentialities, into the field of possible future effects. Now, focus your attention on the image that makes you feel alive, balanced, and at peace. Stay there; allow the feelings raised by that possibility to permeate

---

37. Vaidyanathan, V. (2022, July 8). What is the observer effect in quantum mechanics? *Science ABC*. https://www.scienceabc.com/pure-sciences/observer-effect-quantum-mechanics

your present state of mind. If you stay there long enough, numerous things will happen. First, you will collapse the quantum wave, turning a potentiality into an actuality, creating something more tangible than just a possible scenario. Then, that quantum wave will be captured, shifting from wave energy, or potentiality, into particles, or matter. Your thoughts will transform something that existed only as a possibility into something actual; they will transform an abstraction into a fact, an idea into a thing.

Next, because your brain can't immediately tell whether your thoughts are factual or not, your intentional focus on an image or idea of a happy, healthy you will send the message of happiness to your brain, which will respond as if that imagined future happiness and health are here-and-now fact. Your brain will relax, lowering cortisol and increasing dopamine and perhaps oxytocin (depending on what you are thinking about).

As you can see, our thoughts direct our emotional and physiological reality in a very direct and concrete way. Who knew we had so much power?

This same principle holds true for not only the small-scale, day-to-day details of how we think and therefore feel, but also for the bigger picture, ultimately determining the direction of our lives. We become resonant to those things we desire; we become a match for that potentiality. When we're feeling happy and optimistic, we're more likely to make the choices that align with the things we want, and thus move us directly toward them.

However, it's never really about those *things*, is it?

There are some pervasive and misleading beliefs about vision, achievement, outcomes, and getting the "thing." I had a call the other day with a formidable client who created his first ever vision board. He is already successful, but he is ready for a bigger vision, for more. His vision board was inspiring: he envisioned himself owning golf courses, private jets, and incredible mansions, and speaking in front of thousands of people. Honestly, I have no doubt that he will actually do all of these things (one of those clients), but I asked him a question: Suppose you get all of these "things." Would that make you happy? He answered with a resounding *yes*. How long would that happiness last? I asked. He said, "Maybe a few months, and then I would want more."

Bingo.

THEREIN LIES YOUR ESCAPE FROM THE PRISON OF NEVER ENOUGH

Therein lies your escape from the prison of never enough: You will never stop wanting more. The fallacy lies in always wanting more, and in believing that the "thing" we want will make us happy. What will make us happy is becoming the person who is standing in front of all those people because of what it took to get there and how we evolved and grew on our way to that point.

Even if we are not "there" yet, wherever we imagine "there" to be, we are now at a point that we once saw as a goal. Remember that? At one time, my main goal in life was to finish college in America, make my parents proud, and make $10 an hour so I could send money back home. That was my *dream* at one point. Needless to say, that no longer suffices; but I did that. It's natural to want more for ourselves, our families, and our lives. However, the greatest gift I have given to myself is the steady, constant awareness that I have already arrived. I already have everything I have ever wanted. Wanting more can serve as inspiration; it can encourage us to grow and expand. However, I have already arrived. That awareness affords me an inner peace that closes the loop of constant striving. It removes me from the constant cycle of not-enough-ness because I don't have the "thing."

WE CREATE OUR REALITY WITH EVERY THOUGHT; AND EVERY THOUGHT AFFECTS THE QUALITY OF OUR LIFE

We create our reality with every thought; and every thought affects the quality of our life. We can collapse the quantum wave. By becoming more conscientious about the way we view our thoughts, feelings, and lives, by becoming more intentional observers of those things, we can create a vastly more desirable, and hopeful, effect.

" *When we daydream, we collapse waves of energy and turn them into something real; we turn potentiality into an actuality. This is the act of building a quantum bridge.*

Envision: Building a Quantum Bridge

The source and center of all man's creative power—the power that above all others lifts him above the level of brute creation, and that gives him dominion over all the fish of the sea, the birds of the air, and the animals that move and creep on the earth—is his power of making images, or the power of the imagination.

—Glen Clark, *The Soul's Sincere Desire*

Daydreaming all along

When I was growing up, we had a dog named Linda—a cool American name, we thought. After the war, everyone seemed to be dragging, but not Linda. She was always so happy to see me and excited when I would pay any attention to her. In Bosnia, we kept dogs outside, chained to old wooden dog houses, even during the winter.

I didn't like that. I would often take Linda for walks to a nearby hill where she could run free. I told Linda everything. She would run around, burn off all her excess energy and excitement, and then come sit next to me. Together, we would look down at the city from the hilltop.

It was such a small city. I wondered why I was living there and I wondered if there was a lesson in it all. I dreamed of a better future. Even though there was no Internet and I had very little exposure to the outside world, as I sat on the hill with Linda, I would allow myself to dream of more exciting things: faraway lands where I would feel safe, having all the books I wanted to read, wearing nicer clothes, and most of all, being free. There was always something appealing about going to the United States of America—a bastion of freedom, safety, and possibility. These were far-fetched dreams, I knew, but it felt good to imagine it anyway. Linda would look at me with her sad eyes and her tongue sticking out. She didn't say, "Girl, you just came out of a refugee camp, stop with that nonsense." It was almost as if she was dreaming with me. Much of my life was very, very hard; dreaming made me feel better.

I can see now that daydreaming allowed me to imagine the life I have today, and ultimately, it gave me the tools I would need to build it. Everything I imagined back on that hilltop with Linda came true. The reality of this life far exceeds even my imagination.

In fact, I was collapsing that quantum wave, turning my dreams into something very real: a quantum bridge.

Your future self is already here

The clearest example of the observer effect is light.

Light takes only two forms: it exists as either a wave or a particle. This is referred to as the "wave/particle duality." When a light photon is not being observed, it exists in waveform; but at the moment of observation, the wave collapses and becomes a particle. It takes nothing more than observation to collapse the wave and transform the nature of light from energetic potentiality to material reality; it becomes "something" only when it is observed.

When we daydream, we collapse waves of energy and turn them into something real; we turn potentiality into an actuality. This is the act of building a quantum bridge. Although we are often told to get real and stop daydreaming, the truth is that daydreaming—imagining a future in which we have realized the potential for good things to occur—is a creative act, and has real, material effects. It's turning thoughts into things.

> **WHEN WE DAYDREAM, WE COLLAPSE WAVES OF ENERGY AND TURN THEM INTO SOMETHING REAL**

Now, let's consider how most of us "daydream." We ruminate about the things that didn't go well, we perseverate about worst-case scenarios, we seek out reasons to doubt, hesitate, and fear. When we do this, the very same laws of physics apply—we're just allowing them to play out in a way that does not serve us. In fact, we're building quantum bridges that lead us straight to things we do not want.

Physicist Henry Stapp[38] sees the physical world as a structure of tendencies or probabilities that exist within the world of the mind. Stapp holds that the mind is a real physical structure in which all things exist as possibilities, as potential. Selecting one possibility from among these many is made by conscious choice—not by chance. Stapp believes the physical world is nothing more than one mental structure among an infinite number of possible worlds. We see the world as having a single, concrete actuality because our consciousness selects one possibility from among many. Therefore, reality is not objective but subjective, a structure created by the mind. If it is correct, Stapp says, quantum theory shows that consciousness plays an active role in constructing the physical world.

---

38. Stapp, H. (2011). *Mindful Universe: Quantum Mechanics and the Participating Observer* (2nd ed.). Springer.

At the very least, the willingness to imagine a positive outcome for yourself and for the world, for your happiness and your health, is both a creative and a constructive act in everyday life. We should not only daydream daily but also encourage our children and everyone around us to use this practice. The more we do it, and the more consistent we become at it, the more it becomes a habit that creates our lives.

Live it List™

Nicole Middendorf[39] is a wealth advisor, coach, public speaker, and creator of the "Live it List." It's her version of a bucket list: doing one thing a month that she really wants to do. When I talked to her, she spoke about how life-changing this practice was and how much fuller her life has been since she began to employ it. However, it was born as an antidote to fear.

Nicole is a survivor of domestic violence, an experience that suffused her life with fear to such an extent that it took years for her to emerge—but emerge she did.

Healing, Nicole tells me, "did not come easy." She saw a therapist, read a lot of books, gave it time; and she tried to identify the ways in which fear was affecting her entire life.

"I sat down one night," Nicole says, "My kids were really little. My daughter was six months old, and my son was only two. And I'm like, how did I end up in this place? And how do I get out of it? And so that's the question. If you have fear, where is it coming from? What's going to work for you? What are you going to do about it?"

More than anything else, Nicole says, she decided to start tearing down the limits that fear had placed on her life.

She decided she was going to rewrite her bucket list and do one thing on it every month. To neutralize fear and take back her life,

---

39. Middendorf, N. (n.d.). Live it list. https://nicolemiddendorf.com/live-it-list/

she shifted her focus, creating the "live it list" that now inspires her and others to live the lives they want—not later, but here and now.

Bucket lists and live it lists alike are creative acts—they require our effort, our dreams, and our vision to come true. I have so many items on my own list that **BUCKET LISTS AND LIVE IT LISTS ALIKE ARE CREATIVE ACTS** are 10 or even 20 years away, but by putting them on my list, I am reminded of them, I look forward to them, and most important, I am inspired to take the steps necessary to make them a reality. Stone by stone, I start building a quantum bridge.

As chaotic and incomprehensible as life may seem sometimes, we have far more control over its direction—and our own—than we think. Even a bad strategy poorly executed will take us farther than if we just allow life to toss us around like a bottle in the sea. Every great achievement in this world owes something to the creative spark of an idea, and the strategy that brought about the desired effects. However, before we create a strategy, we need to identify the idea, the creative spark; we need to envision what it is that we really want. This is paramount. So much of our inner turmoil comes from not living our lives, but finding ourselves pulled into other people's lives,

---

Exercise: Write a "live it list" or bucket list

Start by writing down things that you are looking forward to next year and then adding some long-term dreams that still feel just like dreams. Here are some examples from Nicole's "live it list": "Go in a submarine. Ride an elephant. Go to South America. Pet a tiger." One item on my list: to one day have a beautifully manicured European garden with boxwood and hydrangeas. These are funny, inspiring, and interesting examples, and we are all going to have different things we want to do. Make sure your list is honest and authentic to you.

responding to someone else's expectations, our efforts and energy co-opted for the purpose of pursuing someone else's dreams.

Daydreaming is powerful. How do we gain clarity about our lives and envision the future we want?

Dream away

Albert Einstein famously said, "Imagination is more important than knowledge. For knowledge is limited to all we now know and un-

> **"LOGIC WILL GET YOU FROM A TO B. IMAGINATION WILL TAKE YOU EVERYWHERE."**

derstand, while imagination embraces the entire world, and all there ever will be to know and understand." He also said, "Logic will get you from A to B. Imagination will take you everywhere."

The dictionary defines imagination as, "the act or power of forming a mental image of something not present to the senses or never before wholly perceived in reality." Daydreaming is a vital part of the creative process. Someone who daydreams has a creative, agile, and open mind. Allowing the mind to wander freely creates space for new ideas, and it allows connections to emerge in ways that they don't when we are locked into more linear thought patterns, let alone when our thought life is fragmented and frayed by distraction, incoherence, and the chaotic churn of imbalance and stress in our lives. The ability to imagine something different from our immediate reality leads to artistic and intellectual creation, scientific and technological invention and innovation, and personal and social evolution—in short, all forms of progress and change.

Imagination is the one of the most powerful tools you have. An inspiring vision backed by a strategic plan can turn a mediocre company into a powerhouse; it can turn a decent idea into a world-changing innovation. It's the difference between winning and losing, between thriving and floundering.

This world is much more malleable and yielding than we often think it is. Our task is first to imagine the world in which we want to live, and then to create it.

THIS WORLD IS MUCH MORE MALLEABLE AND YIELDING THAN WE OFTEN THINK IT IS

Tennis player Novak Djokovic, a man who has achieved a rare pinnacle of success in the world of sports, used to struggle. An incredible athlete, even he used to get in his own way. In a 2015 interview, he told the *New York Times*[40] that visualization played a significant role in his eventual success. He described envisioning a hoped-for future as a type of meditation, clarifying that he doesn't meditate as an escape from problems, but as a means of creating a mental picture of the future he wants to achieve, grounding his efforts to achieve it in practical actions and illuminating the steps along the path he needs to take. "I strongly believe in visualization," he said. "I believe that there is a law of attraction: You get the things that you produce in your thoughts. Life just works that way." Although we might scoff at the simplicity of his words or assume that he doesn't understand our specific situation, the truth is that almost every success story involves a person with a vision, a hope, a dream.

So how do we do this, and what does it look like? Once you have clarity about what you want, it's time to start envisioning a life where that dream has come true.

For example, if your dream is to be a full-time writer, what would that look like? What does your day entail? What are you doing? How do you feel? What would your income look like? Furthermore, and equally important, what *isn't* a part of that life? What would you say no to? What actions, choices, and attitudes don't align with your dream? Maybe you would be working from home, writing in solitude with no distractions. If so, you would have the freedom to write

---

40. Clarey, C. (2015, September 14). Novak Djokovic's winning strategy: Mind over chatter. *New York Times.* https://www.nytimes.com/2015/09/15/sports/tennis/novak-djokovics-winning-strategy-mind-over-chatter.html

whenever you wanted and could take vacations at any time. Your work would get published in magazines, newspapers, and other publications regularly. What else? What are the things that matter most to you in this vision of yourself? How does this vision make you feel?

IF YOU ENVISION BEING A FAMOUS WRITER WITHOUT THE WRITING, THAT'S JUST A FOOL'S ERRAND

The more detailed and the clearer you are about what you want, the easier it is to create it. When you have a clear picture of what you want your life to look like, it's easier to make decisions that move you toward this vision. That said, if you envision being a famous writer without the writing, that's just a fool's errand. Dreams and anything similar that are worth building require that we show up for that work and take necessary actions that will get us there. Anyone who has built something great knows that this takes time and effort.

Exercise: Clean the mirror

Once we remove the noise from our lives and begin to reflect, we can ask ourselves a few questions.

- What do I really want?
- Whose expectations am I fulfilling?
- What would make me truly happy?
- If I were to start over, what would I do?
- What does my ideal life look like?
- What is my vision?

Write it out. If you're a visual person, create a vision board. Cut out or print images and words that inspire you as a physical reminder of your vision. Keep it close, bless it, look at it often and imagine yourself having "arrived."

To access a clear creative vision, Dr. Nisha Manek points out, "You have to clean the mirror." We need silence; we need to stem (if not totally stop) the flood of information we're taking in. "We have to unplug from that," she says, and continues,

> It's okay. You're not missing a single thing now. You have the potential to create something of your own. Your imagination is activated, and your creativity can come in many ways. It can come in baking a chocolate chip cookie, or it can come through a written proposal for your business. Ultimately, you want to serve. You can get there. Clean out your mirrors, go into silence, and imagine it.

Who are you and what do you want?

Why do you do what you do? What's your endgame? What happens when you get everything you want? If you haven't thought about these things, now is the time. You need a clear vision of your future and an end goal that can motivate you through life's ups and downs. When you have clarity about your goal, it's easy to see the steps you need to take right now to reach it. You can also see when you're getting off course and adjust accordingly. The following is an example of how this works. Let's say you want to lose weight. You can have an end goal of fitting into a certain clothing size, but a more specific vision of what it will feel like when you reach your goal can inspire you in a way a clothing size or number on the scale never can. What will your clothes feel like when they fit properly? How will you feel when you look in the mirror? What sort of activities will you be able to do? Who will notice the difference?

It's surprising how few people are clear about where they are going. However, we need direction. It's likely that you type in the address of your destination into one of your apps when heading to

"I ALWAYS WANTED TO BE SOMEBODY. I GUESS I SHOULD HAVE BEEN MORE SPECIFIC." a new place. Before you take the first step, you have to know where you are headed. I am always surprised to hear people say they have no idea what they want out of life, or claim they are just "going with the flow." As Lily Tomlin said, "I always wanted to be somebody. I guess I should have been more specific."

Sometimes I think we have forgotten that our days are our own; we hold our lives in our hands.

Exercise: Imagine your future self

Close your eyes and imagine a version of yourself that is healthy, happy, wealthy, in a relationship, or whatever else you desire. Stay in that place for a few moments every day. You are building a quantum bridge. For all of the things you don't believe you can have or are afraid to even dream of, just ask *what if?* What if I actually did this? What if it worked? This is a powerful exercise that allows you to face your fears and identify your limiting beliefs.

Strategize your life

When we've cleared a space in the chaos of our lives, created coherence in ourselves, and allowed ourselves to envision the details of the life of our dreams, it's time to *do*.

Mike Paton, an award-winning speaker and author, who teaches practical tools that help leaders and entrepreneurs get unstuck, tells me this:

I have a crystal-clear vision for my business and my life, and it's written down, and I know what my core values are. I know what I want to accomplish in life, both for my family and for my business. I have a set of behavioral norms or execution norms that I want to stick with. I'm able to use those clearly defined anchors, for lack of a better term, or pillars, as a source of the right answer or right decision when I'm stressed and troubled and unsure of myself.

What Mike does so well and teaches others to do is have a vision to rely on in hard times. When we get overwhelmed, we move into survival mode. Not having a vision, he says, is like, "trying to paint your house while it's on fire." Life will undoubtedly present challenges, but if we know where we are headed, it's easier to make decisions. As Mike puts it, "The worst decision you can make is almost always no decision at all."

> "THE WORST DECISION YOU CAN MAKE IS ALMOST ALWAYS NO DECISION AT ALL."

There are many possibilities at every moment in our lives. None of them are fixed. The outcome has more to do with our perception, its narrowness or breadth, than anything else. We truly create our own reality all the time.

CHAPTER 7

Recontextualize: Seeing Things in a New Way

By looking at only one place, you miss everything in all the other places! Look everywhere to see everything!

—Mehmet Murat İldan

"What's the point?" I angrily asked my mom when she woke me up and made me clean the house with her. "War is raging, Dad is gone, and you want me to scrub the floors. What the hell?"

"Just get dressed; breakfast is on the table," she said as she pulled the sheets off me.

Every Saturday morning, she would strip the sheets, open the windows, and wake us up to deep clean the house. Ask any teenager how they feel being woken up early, add manual labor, and you get the picture.

"War may be going on, but it doesn't mean we have to live like pigs," she would say as she moved from the bathroom to the living room, never stopping for a minute.

I hated Saturday mornings.

"Mama, it's freezing," I would say while trying to get dressed.

"You will be just fine. A little fresh air won't kill you."

"Why do we have to wake up so early? Why can't we sleep in like the other kids?"

"Because the sooner you start, the sooner you can enjoy the fruits of your labor."

"I don't care about having a clean house," I said.

"You don't now, but you will in a few hours," she continued, putting on her favorite folk music and bringing warm milk to the breakfast table.

"There. Now you eat so we can get started."

The first hour was a pissing match with teenagers being teenagers, but the brisk movement along with music made me truly happy. It felt good to be doing this and seeing progress. The product was crispness, freshness, newness, and an overwhelming feeling that everything was going to be okay. I remember one time when I pulled the crisp white linens off the line on a hot summer day and I buried my head in them. Oh, heavens! Pots bubbled in the kitchen; lunch was almost ready. It was an orchestra. Cleaning, laundry, cutting meat, washing windows, and adding rice to chicken.

I remember one time after we were done, we sat down and admired our work.

"Now, doesn't that feel nice?" Mama asked.

"Yes. You are right. But Mama, I don't want to spend my life being a wife who cleans. I don't want your life." Saying it felt harsh.

"CLEANING DOESN'T MAKE YOU ME. IT'S JUST IMPORTANT. IT'S DIGNITY."

"You will never have my life. My life is my life and I have made peace with it, but you? You will do great things. Just keep studying like I told you."

"Do you really think so, Mama?"

"I know so. But cleaning doesn't make you me. It's just important. It's dignity."

My mother's life was very difficult, yet very common in a patriarchal country where women traditionally took the roles of homemaker, mother, and very obedient wife. She did not have the luxury of thinking much about herself, but her love for others kept her from wallowing in sadness or complaining that her life was unfair. The world treated her unkindly, but she kept going—and she remembered to do something, even one small thing, that made her a queen for the day.

Although her life offered her precious little dignity, my mother found ways to maintain and sustain herself. She loved cleaning. It made her feel powerful and in control. She was always in good spirits when she cleaned. Even during war, even living a life that at times was pure hell, come Saturday morning, my mother cleaned, and in this way, she became the ray of sunshine we needed—and she needed—in a gloomy world. By claiming ownership of this one space in her world and this one aspect of her life, she brought beauty and order to them both. That effort to recontextualize gave her power.

Recontextualize

To recontextualize means to place something in a different context to suggest a different interpretation. Recontextualizing allows us to see things differently, redefining and reimagining our situations in ways that reveal new angles, new implications, and new truths.

My teacher Steven introduced me to the power of recontextualization. It is the foundation of his practice

TO RECONTEXTUALIZE MEANS TO PLACE SOMETHING IN A DIFFERENT CONTEXT TO SUGGEST A DIFFERENT INTERPRETATION

of Whisperology, and it continues to be a guiding principle in my daily life. Recontextualization is an expansion of context: By reframing what we see, it changes our perception, and thus transforms the meaning of what we see.

I cannot say I had a happy childhood. I grew up in a war zone, lived in a refugee camp, and was raised in a time of severe economic hardship. Nothing was easy. At times, it seemed there was nothing to look forward to. However, my mother created a different reality for us. There was bread to make, there were sheets to wash, there were kids to feed. She took control of what little she could, and she poured her energy and dedication into that, resolving to have the cleanest house ever and the best food for her family.

Growing up, there was no escaping the stark reality that my country was at war. Why clean? For my mother, cleaning was a means of maintaining her sanity; it shifted her focus from one aspect of reality to another, providing her with a sense of purpose and meaning as well as reminding her—and us—that there was still something for which we could be grateful, something to hold onto in dark times. It didn't change the reality of war, but it transformed one area of our lives, reminding us of our humanity, of the necessity of order, and of the power to create change—both within and without—through simple acts.

"THERE'S NOTHING LIKE SLEEPING IN CRISP, CLEAN, FRESHLY PRESSED LINENS"

Even now, I get on my hands and knees and clean every inch of my house when I'm stressed or when things don't look good. It is cathartic, and it directs my energy in a way that is purposeful and gives me concrete, pleasing results. "There's nothing like sleeping in crisp, clean, freshly pressed linens," Mama would say. She taught me to savor those small, wonderful things, those pleasures that still existed in the hell hole of the war into which I was born. Maybe that's why I'm so adamant about how there's always some good in any situation. It truly is a matter of perspective.

Let's say I have the most miserable day ever: my kids are fighting, I get into an argument with my husband, I have a headache, I spill coffee on my blouse on my way to work. I can still come home, take the time to put fresh sheets on the bed, and climb in, grateful that I have clean sheets. It seems laughable, small, and insignificant if I allow the stressors of "real" life to sway me, but that process of refocusing and recontextualizing—for example, by attending to aspects of real life that bring us pleasure, joy, and peace—changes the way our brain works, how we see things, and how we feel.

All around the world, people are caught in horrifying situations; yet many of them still manage to hold on to something that makes them hopeful, something that makes them smile. It doesn't mean they are living in denial; they too experience suffering, defeat, and pain. However, it does mean they can connect with or hold on to something that brings them solace in hard times, reminds them of the possibility of peace and joy, and that uplifts them. We can learn from them, recontextualizing our experience and subsequently, our lives.

Whatever we focus on grows. If we focus on fear, we see and feel more of it, and in turn, we become more fearful. We teach ourselves to see everything through that filter; it shapes our perception of ourselves, of others, of the world; it influences our thoughts and controls our feeling; and it drives our actions and decisions—when we see the world from a place of fear, we actually create a world in which fear rules. Likewise, when we focus on the good things in our lives, we create a world and a way of being that is guided by principles of that goodness, whatever that is for us.

> **WHATEVER WE FOCUS ON GROWS**

I'm not saying negative things don't happen, of course they do. I am saying that we have more control over our experience than we often believe we do. We are much stronger than we think. Steve explained this to me as seeing life through a wide-angle lens; the shift in perspective alone changes the meaning of what we see. When I look at everything close up—every feeling, every disturbance, every concern—I lose perspective altogether. When I pull the camera back to get a look at the big picture, I see not only the truths I'd lost sight of but also all my problems are brought down to size.

The observer effect

Victor Frankl, a Holocaust survivor and author of *Man's Search for Meaning*,[41] writes, "Between stimulus and response, there's a space. In that space is our power to choose our response. In our response lives our growth and our freedom."

Although this is life wisdom all of us could heed, it's more than that as well. Quantum physics shows that we influence the behavior of atoms through observation. In a very concrete way, reality *is* what we choose to observe. Neale Donald Walsh[42] famously said,

REALITY *IS* WHAT WE CHOOSE TO OBSERVE

"It means that everyone sees a different truth, because everyone is creating what they see."

In the early 1900s, physicists discovered something fascinating: Subatomic particles seem to appear and disappear, apparently existing in several dimensions at once. The particles' behavior at the quantum level was a mystery—why did they move in a particular way, take different forms, or appear in one dimension rather than another?—until scientists determined the common causal factor: The particles behaved differently when they were being observed.

The discovery of the observer effect vastly increased our understanding of how the human mind filters and organizes the information that reaches us, from how it interprets the constant onslaught of simultaneous sensation to how it misunderstands social cues and

41. Frankl, V. (2006). *Man's Search for Meaning*. Beacon Press.
42. Walsch, N. D. (2010). *When Everything Changes, Change Everything: In a Time of Turmoil, a Pathway to Peace*. Hodder Paperbacks.

how it comprehends math. This proves there is no such thing as an objective reality; instead, everything exists in a state of "potentiality" until it's observed—and even then, our perception

EVERYTHING EXISTS IN A STATE OF "POTENTIALITY" UNTIL IT'S OBSERVED

of reality is wholly subjective, shaped and created by the way we see.

There are many possibilities at every moment in our lives. None of them are fixed. The outcome has more to do with our perception, its narrowness or breadth, than anything else. We truly create our own reality all the time.

This means that we participate in determining the quality of our lives, in the present as well as the future. That is incredibly empowering. While scientific findings show us *how* this works, mystics and sages have suspected that we have held this power all along. What did they know or see? How do we tap into what they know?

The poet Rumi wrote, "You were born with potential. You were born with goodness and trust. You were born with ideals and dreams. You were born with greatness. You were born with wings. You are not meant for crawling, so don't. You have wings. Learn to use them and fly."[43]

He wrote this, too: "Do you know what you are? You are a manuscript of a divine letter. You are a mirror reflecting a noble face. This universe is not outside of you. Look inside yourself; everything that you want, you are already that."[44]

Quantum theory transformed the scientific understanding of reality and the way it works. As Gloria Prema writes,

Relativity (sometimes called determinism because in it the future is already determined) describes the large scale. It's the

---

43. Rumi, J. (2022). *Rumi: Drop of Enlightenment.* Independently published
44. Rumi, J. (1999). *Hush, Don't Say Anything to God: Passionate Poems of Rumi.* Jain Publishing Company.

Divine blueprint or master plan, if you like, because past, present, and future all exist simultaneously. This means that the future is already determined. It has already happened, in other words. Relativity tells us that there is no point in making any choices because the future is already there. It's already known. So, in effect, we have no free will.

However, she writes that quantum theory has changed all that, showing that,

> Not only is the future not fixed, but even each subatomic particle is unpredictable and we force it to make a choice as to where and when it will manifest by observing it. This is the same as saying that thought creates reality. It is saying that we have free will and it is by making choices that we choose our reality.[45]

Every time we imagine our future with intention, we collapse the quantum wave; we shape our future and make choices about the direction it will take. Theoretical physicist Werner Heisenberg, a pioneer in the field of quantum mechanics, famously said, "Atoms are not things, they are only tendencies. Atoms or elementary particles themselves are not real; they form a world of potentialities or possibilities rather than one of things or facts."[46]

EVERY TIME WE IMAGINE OUR FUTURE WITH INTENTION, WE COLLAPSE THE QUANTUM WAVE; WE SHAPE OUR FUTURE AND MAKE CHOICES ABOUT THE DIRECTION IT WILL TAKE

Think about it this way: Our whole world is made up of

---

45. Prema, G. (2022). *It's All Light: Juicy Science Meets Spirituality Without Religion*, p. 60. Independently Published.
46. Heisenberg, W. (n.d.). *Quotes*. Goodreads. https://www.goodreads.com/quotes/896047-t-he-atoms-or-elementary-particles-themselves-are-not-real-they

atoms. The events, the environments, the people—all atoms. However, Heisenberg says, atoms are tendencies, possibilities, not fixed and final things; in fact, they are dormant until we place our focus on them. For every unfortunate event that happens in our lives, there is also a potential reality in which that never happened. Say I am sick, and in that moment, there are multiple possibilities/potentialities in my future. There is also a situation/case in which I am not sick.

The universe continually unfolds from a state of potential, known in quantum physics as superposition, where all possibilities exist as part of an underlying field. In this superposition, everything is possible, and nothing actually happens until we observe it.

What does this mean for us? Well, in a word, everything. Science isn't just about observing external things, objects, phenomena, and events; it's also about observing ourselves. This observation—of our thoughts, feelings, emotions, interactions with other people and with the environment, and actions in and responses to situations—can become an intentional practice for us, one that allows us to recontextualize, reimagine, and recreate our lives.

Everything in our reality exists as potential, known in quantum physics as superposition, where all possibilities exist as part of an underlying field. In this superposition, everything is possible, and nothing actually happens until we observe it. A positive outcome for any situation already exists as a possibility in the quantum field; a positive outcome in your life is there, waiting to be imagined, or observed, by you. Your focus on it makes it a reality.

> **EVERYTHING IN OUR REALITY EXISTS AS POTENTIAL, KNOWN IN QUANTUM PHYSICS AS SUPERPOSITION**

Recontextualize right now

"It just is, it's not good or bad." This statement always helps me to stay calm. Things that happen are not necessarily bad or good; they just are. Our minds will perceive things differently and the meaning we give them is the meaning they will have. Then I take it a step further by seeking a positive interpretation: "How could this be happening *for* me and not *to* me? Could this be a good thing? What can I learn from this?"

Learning to recontextualize and making it a practice takes time. I don't expect people in pain or intense fear to instantly forget or ignore real distress. However, if we want to live a life that is not controlled by our environment and our collective fear, we owe it to ourselves and each other to strengthen this muscle and begin to exercise our power. We are strong and resilient, and we are in a position to change reality in the world we share.

What is "real" to us is always a projection of our inner world, our state of consciousness. We see the world not as it is but as we are. Fear in particular emerges from a troubled place in the self. Projected into the world, fear creates trouble wherever it goes, moving outward from its source—us—like ripples from a pebble dropped in a pond. This is why the most powerful and necessary recontextualization work we can do is internal: Just as we set waves of fear in motion when we ourselves proceed from fear, we can set other things, other states of consciousness in motion in the world as well—such as peace, kindness, and love.

Steve puts it this way:

Quantum mechanics gives some clues about how we are participants in that which we experience. [Quantum theory] is a means to help us appreciate that it is an illusory and limiting belief that we are separate from the world in which we live. Reality and truth are subjective forms of experience, not simply propositions. Recontextualization is not just a trick to cope with our difficulties but actually transforms life—our lives as well as the lives of others, even the planet. Recontextualization brings order, coherence, and the energy for healing.

> "RECONTEXTUALIZATION IS NOT JUST A TRICK TO COPE WITH OUR DIFFICULTIES BUT ACTUALLY TRANSFORMS LIFE"

Quit limiting yourself with acronym disabilities

I must include a note here about self-talk and labels. I have observed a concerning trend: There is a growing number of people who are self-diagnosing mental and emotional ailments, giving themselves labels, fitting themselves into categories of pathology, and generally telling themselves and others stories that hurt their potential for a better future: I have [insert self-diagnosis]. I am always late. I am a lazy person. That's just the way I am. These labels are limiting and by affirming them on a daily basis, memorizing them, and convincing ourselves of them, we ensure they will stick around.

This is an instance of *building the wrong quantum bridge*.

Danish philosopher Soren Kierkegaard famously wrote, "When you label me, you negate me." For me, this

> "WHEN YOU LABEL ME, YOU NEGATE ME."

means that if you label me, you limit me. You make me less than who I am. You confine me to the traits that fit into that label, stripping away the full breadth of who I am and the range of potentialities for who I could be. It's no different with our children. When we label them, we negate and limit them, confining their true potential to a narrow little list of things someone else—perhaps ourselves—believe they can be. It's important to remember that no label, no matter how well intentioned, is ever comprehensive; as such, it is never entirely true. Labels are simply a way to categorize people and things so that we can understand our world better. However, when we label someone as "the smart one" or "the funny one" or "the troublemaker," we blind ourselves to who they really are, to their full potential and what they can contribute to this world if only given the chance.

How do you label and describe yourself to yourself or others? What if you were to acknowledge the behaviors but imagine a different possibility for yourself? What if you could create a new story for yourself? A story that reflects your values and your purpose, rather than just accepting the labels others have given you, or those that feel comforting because they give you an easy shorthand for explaining and understanding the true ambiguity and nuance of what makes you who you are?

What if you were to acknowledge that you have a pattern of behavior, but are not destined to stay in that pattern?

What if you were to reframe those labels or descriptions and focus not on how they make you a victim but on how they make you

How is this happening *FOR* me, rather than *TO* me?

a person who has endured and survived?

Exercise: How is this happening *for* me, rather than *to* me?

Consider a situation in your life and write it out in a new light, a new way: recontextualize it. What's good or positive in this situation? Write it out in your journal and start telling that story.

Welcome small discomforts and disappointments daily

Yes, these are challenging times. Yes, many wrongs exist. Yes, we are still adjusting to a new and rapidly changing world, but this can still be the best of times, if we shift our perspective so we can see the opportunities this era has raised. To begin, we need simply to ask, "How do I see the good?"

I am all too familiar with things that are measurably, objectively bad; I know the blows life can deal. I know what it's like to live in existential fear, facing the real possibility that any day might be my last, when dodging snipers is an actual thing or when, if you don't run fast enough, a missile could mean your death.

The truth is that we will always face challenges, and in spite of our best efforts and deepest desires, we will face disappointments. To expect anything else is foolish. Even the most committed realists seem crushed and surprised when things go wrong. Often, it's the people who hold onto hope no matter what who show a steady resilience when tragedy strikes. So much of this is perspective; but it's not enough to just say it. We have to believe it, live it, and strengthen that muscle, little by little, every day. We have to decide to flip the switch intentionally and activate the observer effect.

It's likely that every day will contain a multitude of micro-disappointments for all of us. By acknowledging them and focusing on what good can be found in each situation, we teach ourselves the valuable skill of flexibility; we become as supple as trees in the fall when the wind starts to blow, causing them to toss and bend.

I like the imagery of trees for humans. Deeply rooted, solid, yet flexible and yielding to outside forces. If trees were more rigid, the sheer force of wind would tear them down. You are the tree. We all are. We too are strong and deeply rooted and we can withstand just about anything in life. I know; I have seen people survive the unimaginable and even thrive.

Welcome small discomforts and disappointments daily. Then, for a brief moment, affirm one thing that is good. Ask yourself: What is something good in my life right now, regardless of this hardship? By repeating the process, we strengthen the neuropathways, eventually training our brains to respond to distress cues with curiosity and gratitude rather than with further distress. This does not mean you become a passive victim of life's whims. It just means you energetically put yourself in a state for a better response to a situation.

Is fear real?

Throughout human history, we have struggled to find a way to maintain inner peace in the midst of discord, hardship, and unrest. It's been a challenge of all of our lives. Fear is so real when we feel it. It paralyzes us, throwing us into a tailspin of anxiety, irrationality, and misguided actions that create more of the very things we don't want.

Fear is anticipating negative and painful outcomes and assuming the worst is to come.

Often, when we feel it, we have to ask ourselves if we are afraid because something is really and truly dangerous, or if we are afraid because we *believe* some danger exists—or even that it *could* exist. Where is the belief coming from? Is it true? Where is our focus? What are we seeing? Our perception of reality—for example, that there is a cause for fear—is invariably shaped by our beliefs, especially by our limiting beliefs. Here, I'm reminded of Steve's words about the power of recontextualization to transform, expand, and overcome limitations. Recontextualization, he says, "changes the conversation."

Despite global chaos, upheaval, and change, this time gives us fertile ground for personal transformation and for creating transformation in the world. As curators of our experience, we must acknowledge that no two of us see the same world in the same way; but we do *share* this world. So, we must choose wisely when we give meaning to something we see.

THIS TIME GIVES US FERTILE GROUND FOR PERSONAL TRANSFORMATION AND FOR CREATING TRANSFORMATION IN THE WORLD

Many of us have heard the story about the two wolves. The version I've heard is from the Cherokee tradition and it involves a father telling his son about the black wolf and the white wolf who were engaged in an endless battle. The son, impatient to know the ending, asked: "Father, which wolf will win?" And the father replied, "Whichever one you feed."

Everything around and in us is energy. Our role is to know that and learn how to create with that energy. Remember, thoughts are energy, things are energy, emotions are energy, music is energy. When we understand this, we can create using that energy with our intention. It's not magic, it's science.

CHAPTER 8

Condition Your Space Like Westminster Abbey: Intention and Physical Space

Energy is what moves our world, our cosmos. Energy is our universal currency, our raw material. There is a law that governs energy. That's thermodynamics in a nutshell.

—Dr. Nisha Manek

I remember walking into a mosque for the first time—a moment I would remember for the rest of my life. My face was covered with a beautifully ironed hijab. The bright, expansive structure was filled with flickering lights. I was overtaken by the feeling that this place gave me, a sense of ceremony and peace. It was so different from the feeling at our house. This was not a joyful time in my life: my father was suffering from unprocessed war trauma, so home was not exactly an oasis of peace.

I sat down quietly in the back row. The hijab covered every strand of my hair; I wore a long skirt and shirt that covered my entire body other than my feet and hands, I closed my eyes and started crying. I couldn't explain it. I wasn't sad. I was overtaken by such a feeling of something—magical? Holy? Peaceful? Happy? I couldn't find a word, but I felt that everything was going to be okay. I felt accepted, safe, and loved; I didn't want to leave. I had never felt that way before that night, but I would feel it again and again over the years, every time I walked into a church, synagogue, or mosque.

THIRTY YEARS LATER, I KNOW WHY THESE SPACES FEEL SO GOOD: PHYSICS.

Thirty years later, I know why these spaces feel so good: physics.

If you've ever had a similar experience or walked into a room where it feels like you could cut the tension with a knife, you're not alone and you're not crazy. Spaces are alive. They carry and store energy just as people do, and they can be influenced by our intention.

"'INTENTION' COMPARED TO 'THOUGHT' IS LIKE COMPARING A LASER BEAM TO A LIGHTBULB. WHILE THEY ARE BOTH LIGHT, ONE CAN CUT THROUGH STEEL AND THE OTHER ILLUMINATES THE ROOM."

"Intention" is both conscious and unconscious. There are the deliberate intentions we know we have; there are also the accidental intentions we create simply by the direction and focus of our thoughts. As the Tiller Foundation website[47] puts it, "'intention' compared to 'thought' is like comparing a laser beam to a lightbulb. While they are both light, one can cut through steel and the other illuminates the room."

Most of us just assume that space is empty, but it is not. Space is filled with information; the nature and intention of that information, in turn, directs the energy within a space.

---

47. Tiller Foundation. (n.d.). Intention Science. https://tillerfoundation.org/

In this chapter, I am going to discuss the science of intention and how we can use it to change our environment, which, like a boomerang, can help change us.

Spaces are alive

There is great power in dedicated spaces; they are constantly being "imprinted" with the intention and vibration of the people who spend time in them. This is why houses of worship often feel sacred; they are imbued with the love and humility of those who gather to worship there.

Dr. Nisha Manek, a board-certified rheumatologist and the author of *Bridging Science and Spirit*,[48] spent the last decade studying the phenomenon of intention. She recalls walking into a small lab in Payson, Arizona. Surrounded by electromagnetic devices, faraday cages, and scientific instruments of all kinds, she was unexpectedly struck by feeling like she had just walked into a space like a high cathedral. "When I was studying in London," she says, "overcome with obligations and stresses of work and life, I would walk into the Abbey and immediately feel at peace. There was something so holy about that place." She was at the lab run by Dr. William Tiller, professor Emeritus of Materials Science and Engineering at Stanford University, hoping to learn more about his discoveries on the power of intention. A medical doctor herself, not a physicist, Dr. Manek sensed Tiller was on to something. She'd requested the opportunity to study with him for years without luck; when he finally accepted, he made one request of her: to meditate daily.

She says this while smiling:

---

48. Manek, N. (2019). *Bridging Science and Spirit: The Genius of William A. Tiller's Physics and Promise of Information Medicine*. Conscious Creation LLC.

Throughout my career and lifetime, I've filled out many application forms. Tell me one place where it says, do you meditate daily? One of the most fundamental skills of a homo sapiens is what? To become familiar with your own mind, your own preferences and prejudices. You need to understand yourself, know yourself. So, when Tiller said, "I want you to meditate daily," I was dumbstruck and delighted. I knew that was it. That's it.

Tiller began his research in the 1960s at Stanford, publishing hundreds of papers and many patents in conventional physics science. At Stanford, Tiller conducted his revolutionary experiments to investigate whether human intention could affect a material. By the time Tiller was drawing up his science protocol, he had been doing daily meditation for more than 25 years. One could say that he was like a scientist sage! His meditation and spiritual practices informed his science. In his life, both aspects were firmly united. His results left little doubt. Intention is a powerful force in nature and influences physical reality.

Tiller discovered something else in his research. Call it Factor X. It was this factor that was the missing piece to the puzzle of enormous effects of intention in his lab. He was the first to notice it and describe and write the equations. The missing piece was the space of the physics laboratory.

We tend to think of space as a vacuum or a void; we think space is just empty space. That's not strictly true. Tiller's work shows that while there is no matter in space, there is always "dense energy potential." That energy is scattered and chaotic. When we introduce intention to this space, that intention or observation changes the behavior of that energy, shifting its nature and creating order (negentropy) where disorder had previously ruled. In a

"HUMAN INTENTION INFLUENCES OR 'COHERES' THE VACUUM STATE TO A MORE ORDERED STATE."

nutshell, Dr. Manek writes, "Human intention influences or 'coheres' the vacuum state to a more ordered state." In *Bridging Science and Spirit*, she explains how this happens in detail.[49]

Tiller utilized something called an intentional host device (IHD) in his experiments, simply because humans cannot maintain one thought or intention for longer periods. I remember trying to imprint water for the first time and how my mind jumped from one thought to another. I have gotten better at doing this, but my mind still moves away from intention after a long period.

Postulating that intention can influence the behavior of matter, Tiller "charged" the IHD with intention and conducted experiments on raising and lowering the pH of water. The results were consistently statistically significant, bearing out what we've seen in earlier chapters: Particles change their state upon being observed, and matter is indeed influenced by intention.

This has immediate implications for our lives. Broadly speaking, it clarifies the law of attraction (or resonance) and helps us understand why—and how—we can alter and direct reality through our intentions and thoughts. In a very concrete and specific way, it tells us how our thoughts and intentions can change the quality of the space we are in, giving us the power to imbue our spaces with the peace that fills Westminster Abbey and the mosque where I found such solace as a young girl. Your home can become a holy and highly conditioned space for you and everyone who enters.

> **YOUR HOME CAN BECOME A HOLY AND HIGHLY CONDITIONED SPACE FOR YOU AND EVERYONE WHO ENTERS**

---

49. In *Bridging Science and Spirit*, Dr. Nisha Manek writes a detailed explanation of the science behind creating what Dr. Tiller called "conditioned" space. Using the science of thermodynamics, she explains how the conditioned spaces are created. I highly recommend reading this book if you are ready to take your understanding of science to an entire new level.

Intentional space

Intention is a very focused thought directing energy toward a specific outcome. For example, if you intend to make your home an oasis of peace where everyone feels welcomed and calm, you have a clear intention with a specific outcome. Now the task is to get ourselves into a good-feeling state and direct our energy toward the intention and outcome we desire. The trouble with the human condition is that we cannot hold a stable intention consistently because most of us are not particularly disciplined with our thoughts and feelings. This is why you should create your own IHD—an item that you can "imprint" with intention, one that can hold and broadcast your intention when you cannot.

"INTENTION IS USING YOUR CONSCIOUSNESS TO EFFECT AN OUTCOME THAT HAS AN IMPACT ON YOUR EVERYDAY LIFE."

Gloria Prema says, "Intention is using your consciousness to effect an outcome that has an impact on your everyday life." Being more intentional about all aspects of our lives will bring vitality, satisfaction, and a sense of purpose; but to begin, we can bring those things into our space.

Let me give you a practical example. The intention statement I have created for my home and my family reads,

> The intention is to create an environment of kindness, love, peace, and the grace of God. This house is being assisted by the Great Unseen. This is a sacred space, and people in this house flourish, increase in consciousness and know faith, possibility, and joy without doubt. And so it is. Thy will be done.

We are not a religious family, but we do believe that a beautiful energy exists and is here to support us and lives in all of us. We call it love.

I wrote that intention out after one of my meditations. I read it out loud to my family, and we agreed that it sounded good to us. Then we got together, held hands, and held that intention in our minds. I placed the writing behind a picture frame in our entry-way. This picture frame and the written intention hold that intention for us in times when we lose our focus or emotional stability. The intention aids us when we become scattered and incoherent, bringing us back into balance in ourselves, our relationships, and our home. Although this may sound silly at first, it is life-altering to take the time to create an intention for your family. For all the parents out there, this will have a profound effect on your little ones.

> **IT IS LIFE-ALTERING TO TAKE THE TIME TO CREATE AN INTENTION FOR YOUR FAMILY**

Dr. Manek says that being specific about our intentions and writing them down is something she learned from Tiller.

> He was very precise about writing [your intention] down. You'll feel a difference. And I will tell you, when you're writing it out, you'll actually say, that doesn't feel quite so right anymore. And just the revision of it tells you you're on the right track, you're prioritizing things. [Tiller] had a spiral notebook he carried in his briefcase, and he would bring it out, and he always wrote down his intentions.

Exercise: Create an intention statement for your home

Write out intention statements for your home and read it with your family. Record it in your own voice and let it play repeatedly while you are gone.

Our thoughts are significant. They create our reality, both within and without; they create the feeling we have in our lives and our homes. You can get a candle and imprint it with a certain intention each day; you can imprint a plant or whatever object you desire. Through your intention and by repetition, you create a lasting, stable, intentional space in which to work and live, a space full of positive energy that you and others will feel. In these spaces, we can allow the ego to quiet down, we can tune out the noise, and we can continue to condition our spaces with love, forgiveness, and hope. The space holds that intention, which affects everyone who walks in.

Energy can be molded but never destroyed. Energy is also neutral; it's neither bad nor good. That said, we all have days when we feel "low" energy or that we are carrying "bad" energy. Our emotions are directly connected to our energy level, so it's natural that after a bad day, we may feel caught in a cycle of negative emotions or a low vibe.

I recently added another sign to our household, intended to remind us that we are each responsible for the energy we bring into the room. What we surround ourselves with matters. When I see that sign, it's a gentle reminder that I have control over my emotional state. Here is what it says:

"PLEASE BE RESPONSIBLE FOR THE ENERGY YOU BRING INTO THIS HOME" Please be responsible for the energy you bring into this home. This is a sacred space. Your words matter. Your behaviors matter. Our family and all who enter this home matter. Take a slow, deep breath and make sure your energy is in check. Thank you. God bless you. You are loved.

It is signed by each member of our family.[50]

---

50. Access to this poster and other customizable intention statement templates for your family is available at www.jasnaburza.com/healerinheels

The other day, my husband and I were in the dining room discussing the different ways we parent. The discussion escalated because the kids came walking in, further supporting what I thought was my righteous claim. In annoyance, I looked away. Guess what caught my eye? You guessed it: "You are responsible for the energy you bring into this room." My ego wanted to be right, but I was putting energy into the room in a way of which I wasn't proud. I was immediately humbled. I wrote down that intention, printed it out, and put it on the wall. It allowed me to reclaim my energy in that moment, and to deescalate a discussion that could have turned ugly. I apologized for getting worked up, excused myself, and went into the backyard to play soccer with the kids and cool off. My intention shifted from wanting to be right to wanting to create a harmonious environment for my children and not ruin their day.

Exercise: Make an inspirational sign

Other than creating an intention statement for your home, be inspired to make a sign that inspires you and place it in a space where you and others will be reminded of it and influenced by it. It could be a poem or rules to live by or anything of the sort.

We do have control over our thoughts and how we show up in this world. This is not toxic positivity; it's a fact, one that can be hard to hear when we are not in a good place, especially when we cannot control our environment. However, over time, as we become more consistent and disciplined in our efforts, we will see tangible results.

We're going to have crappy days; we're going to believe our crappy thoughts and dive into crappy feelings and put our crappy energy into the world. Then, we're going to have the chance—we always do—to change. We must have compassion for ourselves in those moments.

A BAD DAY DOESN'T PRE-VENT YOU FROM GOING HOME AND CREATING AN INTENTIONALLY PEACE-FUL ENVIRONMENT

Part of our journey is in seeing the contrast: Uncomfortable situations and experiences can at least teach us what we *don't* want, and they often inspire us to make a change for the better. A bad day doesn't prevent you from going home and creating an intentionally peaceful environment. In fact, because you have conditioned your space, it will help you recover from the events and emotions that have created the incoherence you feel. As Dr. Manek says while referencing the boomerang idea, "We affect space, and that space affects us."

What are the spaces you want to affect? Home? Work? Garage? What is your intention for each space? Is it to create a meditative place that will allow you to quiet your thoughts and allow your feelings to flow through? An energetic and productive space in which you are inspired, focused, and creating great work? It is up to you; your intention shifts matter, and your intention creates the space.

Exercise: Create an intention statement for specific spaces/rooms in your life

You may have an intention statement for the entire house, but you can also create an intention statement for specific rooms and dwellings: Think of your office where you work, your bedroom, or your garage. What kind of energy do you want to create in those spaces?

As a practical matter, as we begin to condition our spaces, we should remember what we know about simplifying and decluttering. Clutter carries incoherent energy, which we absorb. In contrast, plants improve our mood and raise the vibration of our space. They do so through simple chemistry: increasing oxygen and reducing carbon dioxide, which makes us more energetic. According to a study published in the *Journal of Physiological Anthropology*[51], interaction with indoor plants (like touching and smelling) can reduce physiological and psychological stress. Research shows that plants improve concentration and productivity and boost subjective reports of workers' wellbeing by nearly 50 percent.

My teacher Steve reminds us that we do not fill the space so much as each "living space" permeates us. He says, "The awareness of love that fills space and our own limited presence within the unlimited presence create the experience and power of a sacred space." This is how what we once thought of as an empty space becomes "a healing space."

> **THIS IS HOW WHAT WE ONCE THOUGHT OF AS AN EMPTY SPACE BECOMES "A HEALING SPACE."**

A word of caution: We live in a world where we're led to want and expect instant gratification and immediate results. True, intention can have immediate results. So can a beautiful vase of fresh flowers on a gloomy day. However, to truly condition our spaces, to imprint intentionally and energize them in a deeper and more meaningful way, we should instead create a discipline around this. That's actually good news. Not only does a deliberate practice affirm the value of creating an intentional space, it keeps us mindful of both our intention and its effects, which is the only way to achieve lasting results.

Mahatma Gandhi famously said, "In prayer it is better to have a heart without words than words without a heart." This is true not only in prayer, which we'll discuss next, but in material practice. Tiller's experiments indicate that quieting the mind through meditation and other mindfulness practices, and cultivating a feeling of love and gratitude, make our physical energy more coherent and cohesive, which in

---

51. Lee, M.-S., Lee, J., Park, B.-J., & Miyazaki, Y. (2015). Interaction with indoor plants may reduce psychological and physiological stress by suppressing autonomic nervous system activity in young adults: a randomized crossover study. *Journal of Physiological Anthropology, 34*(21).

turn, heightens the power of our intention and maximizes its effect. We can endeavor to still the mind and emanate positive energy when conditioning our space.

Start with one room: simply create an intention. Maybe you want to start with your bedroom, imbuing it with the energy of a restful oasis. To create that energy, here are just a few things you could do to create that feeling: dim the lights, open the windows each day for fresh air, play soothing music, arrange the furniture so it brings forth calmness, keep the bed made with clean linens that smell good, or remove the TV and all other electronics. Then, set the intention of relaxation every time you enter the space, and ensure that you only sleep and relax in that room. Over time, as your intention is supported by your actions and you condition that space, it becomes the oasis of physical and mental relaxation, restoration, and rest.

By creating and inhabiting intentional spaces, we remind ourselves to utilize intention in every part of our day, from our morning routine to our last conscious thoughts before sleep. You can carry that intention into every segment of your day: from your morning routine to leaving the house. In addition, when coming back from work and still sitting in the car, you can say: "My intention is to let go of the stresses of the day and enter a new family segment where I am present." That's it. That's how simple this can be and how it can help you bring back that energy you desire into your home. If you are having a particularly difficult day, say, "I am just going to breathe today." As Dr. Manek says humorously: "Oh, Lord. Help me shut off the television today." Intention is serious business, but it doesn't have to be grim; its purpose is only to bring harmony and to heal.

OUR INTENTIONS CREATE ORDER IN OUR SPACES, MAKING THEM MORE COHERENT AND ALIGNED WITH US, WHICH BRINGS OUR ENTIRE BODIES INTO A STATE OF COHERENCE

Our intentions create order in our spaces, making them more coherent and aligned with us, which brings our entire bodies into a state of coherence. They affect every aspect of our being, and when we maintain coherence, we find equilibrium, our natural state, and the one in which we can heal, align, and become whole.

These tips may seem obvious to some, while to others, they may seem silly; some are likely familiar ideas, others may be news. Some people will find joy in candles and plants while others will have no desire for these things. The details of how you choose to create your space are less important than that you have a clear intention, a sense of how you want the energy in that space to feel, and what meaning you want it to hold. Consistent intention will help you create an environment in which you and others will thrive. You will change the informational structure of your space, and your space will help you maintain coherence in return. You can create your very own holy place, a sanctuary in which to heal.

YOU CAN CREATE YOUR VERY OWN HOLY PLACE, A SANCTUARY IN WHICH TO HEAL

Everything around and in us is energy. Our role is to know that and learn how to create with that energy. Remember, thoughts are energy, things are energy, emotions are energy, music is energy. When we understand this, we can create using that energy with our intention. It's not magic, it's science.

> *When tough times arrive, they bring with them the opportunity to surrender our beliefs and begin a search for something that can fill the void and heal the pain. A practice to which people have turned throughout human history—one of the most powerful practices in the universe—is prayer. It turns out, science agrees.*

Grandma Was Right, Prayer Works: Directed Intention

For whether we realize it or not, with every breath, with every heartbeat, women pray. One way or another, we pray. Everyday life is the prayer. How we conduct it, celebrate it, consecrate it. It's just that some prayers are better than others. Conscious prayers are the best.

—Sarah Ban Breatnach, *Simple Abundance*

Please God, please... please make sure the grenades don't hit our house. Please, God.

I kept praying. I recited every prayer I knew in Arabic, even though I didn't even know what some of them meant. I just hoped that God would hear me. It was during one of the shelling attacks during the war in Bosnia. I was nine years old. I could hear the grenades falling nearby, followed by a shattering noise: The grenades had hit a home.

"That must have been so-and-so's house," Mama would say.

Normally, the sirens would sound when the shelling started or just before; we would usually have time to hide in the basement or use our better-secured shelters in the neighborhoods. All of us kids knew to run as fast as we could when we heard the pitching sound of a grenade or a siren. *Run for your life* ran through our minds constantly, like a chant. However, this time, it was the middle of the night, and there was no time to run. Our best bet was to hide under the stairs in our house because it was made out of cement. At the time, our reasoning seemed sound; thinking back now, I know that no stairs would have saved us if a grenade had hit our house.

Please, God. Please, God, keep us safe. Please, God. I will do all of my chores without complaining. Please, God, don't let us die tonight.

> **IF YOU KEEP US ALIVE, I WILL NEVER SAY NO TO MAMA AGAIN. PLEASE, GOD.**

Then I said something I will always remember: *If you keep us alive, I will never say no to Mama again. Please, God.*

We survived the shelling. My intention to keep that particular promise faded over time, but I never lost sight of my sense that God had heard and listened to *me*. That night, the grenades hit three homes right around us but not our house. I believed God had something to do with it. It was then that prayer became an integral part of my life.

> **A PRACTICE TO WHICH PEOPLE HAVE TURNED THROUGHOUT HUMAN HISTORY—ONE OF THE MOST POWERFUL PRACTICES IN THE UNIVERSE—IS PRAYER**

When tough times arrive, they bring with them the opportunity to surrender our beliefs and begin a search for something that can fill the void and heal the pain. A practice to which people have turned throughout human history—one of the most powerful practices in the universe—is prayer. It turns out, science agrees.

What is prayer?

What is prayer, and why do we pray? What does it do for us? What if we are not religious? If prayer really does hold some power, how can we tap into that for good? Furthermore, what does science have to do with prayer?

Every religious and spiritual tradition uses some form of prayer or meditation as a foundational practice. From earliest recorded history right up to the present, human beings have found comfort and solace in prayer. For some people, praying requires kneeling and clasping the hand; for others, it involves bowing down in a mosque. The definitions of prayer are as wide-ranging as the practices: prayer is "a devout petition to God" or "a spiritual communion with God or an object of worship, as in supplication, thanksgiving, adoration, or confession."

My healer Steve defines prayer as "a form of directed intention." He says, "We are communicating with a transcendent God but also God within us, the imminent side of God. Prayer is a spiritual intention that recognizes the presence of the divine within us. Petition prayers miss the most important aspects of prayer, which are praise, thanksgiving, and love. Prayer is not about getting what you want; it's about allowing the life force to work in us and through us. That's why the most powerful prayer is, "Not my will, but Thy will be done."

Religion can be controversial, and certainly it's deeply personal; so for the purposes of this book, I will offer my own broad and inclusive definition of prayer: It is an act of an intentional connection to something bigger than ourselves that allows us to surrender to the experience of awe.

We have all had a moment when we have become aware of something larger than ourselves, be that a sense of exquisite beauty, of deep and profound connection, or even of things just being *right*. This, too, is a kind of prayer. For most of my life, prayer was more a state of being than of doing; it was a feeling, a knowing, rather than an act.

As a form of inten-
tion, prayer can be
used in various ways

Prayer is an instinctive response to vulnerability, gratitude, beauty, and pain. It begins as a connection, often when we are suffering, and develops into a creative force that we can learn how to tap into at any time. As a form of intention, prayer can be used in various ways: to heal or get help, to move toward an intended outcome, to offer gratitude, or to ask for guidance and inspiration.

Our grandmothers knew this all along: Prayer affects our physical, mental, emotional, and spiritual health, and it has the power to change our lives. A few years ago, I learned that quantum physics provides a fairly straightforward explanation for how and why prayer works.

The science behind prayer

The belief that there is power behind prayer turns out to have a firm foundation in fact. Advances in quantum theory reveal the existence of something called *entanglement*, which indicates that particles are connected in a mysterious way even when separated. Recalling the observer effect, this means that something that affects a particle's behavior—such as observation—instantly affects other particles with which that one is entangled. This suggests that everything in the universe is indeed intertwined, and that disparate things can influence each other—even if they're very far apart. Some have proposed that prayer is actually an energetic process involving forces we've discussed, including intention, which changes physical matter, and the observer effect.

Let's say you are praying for help. By asking for what you want, you are focusing on a desired outcome and as such, placing more attention and intention on that outcome; the mechanism of the observer effect means that you are lending energy to one of many potentialities and therefore increasing its likelihood of becoming an actuality. The same holds true for a prayer of gratitude: By focusing our attention on something, we are bringing it into our reality and coming into resonance with it. Our thoughts and emotions amplify the effect our focus can have, which we have seen from intention research.

As we know, prayer is notoriously controversial and difficult to study; it does ask us to believe and to surrender to a sense of awe and a recognition of the unknown. Nevertheless, it is a practice that we can make our own, no matter what our position may be on religion, spirituality, and faith. We don't need to be physicists to tap into this power. We don't have to understand the mechanics of electricity to use it daily (and have faith that it will work), do we?

One of the foremost experts on the effectiveness of prayer is Dr. Larry Dossey. His research focuses primarily on our physical wellbeing and the uses of prayer in a medical setting. In his book *Healing Words*[52], Dossey provides an in-depth look at the empirical evidence for the power of intentions to heal remotely—in other words, he studies the effectiveness of prayer. Dossey's research sends a clear message: prayer works. It can help with high blood pressure, asthma, heart attacks, headaches, and anxiety. It can also change enzyme activity, blood cell growth, and seed germination.

My reasoning for bringing up prayer is twofold. First, prayer helps us feel better—physically, mentally, spiritually, and emotionally. It brings us into coherence, which we know positions us to make better choices leading to better results. Second, quantum physics tells us that there is a field that connects us all—the Higgs field, which we'll explore in depth in Part III. If that is true, and if it is true that intention changes physical matter, we can readily see why prayer works.

---

52. Dossey, L. (1995). *Healing Words: The Power of Prayer and the Practice of Medicine.* HarperOne

How do we pray?

PRAYER IS FOCUSED INTENTION, A CRE- ATIVE POWER WE CAN USE TO AID US

Prayer is focused intention, a creative power we can use to aid us. In fact, it is one of the most powerful tools we have for manifesting what we want in life. However, it can be hard to know exactly how to pray.

It's easy to think of prayer as a way to ask for guidance or help and to receive an answer, but there's more to it than that. The following are some tips on how to pray with intention and see results.

Focus on what you want rather than what you don't want. When we focus on what we don't want, we're actually attracting more of that energy into our lives. Instead, focus on what you do want and why it would be good for you. If there's something specific, such as, "I want more money," then ask for guidance on how to earn more money in a way that feels coherent and that aligns with your beliefs.

There are a few broad categories of prayer, each of which can benefit us and bring a different type of energy into the world.

Prayers of supplication: The dark night of the soul

When we pray for help, we often believe that help will arrive in a nicely wrapped package. It will be easy to unpack, and our problem will be solved. In reality, answers and solutions often come in the most painful ways. They come in the form of any illness, of a job loss, or of a huge setback, and we feel the whole world is falling apart.

Emily Ford is one of those people who is larger than life. The moment you meet her, you know you're in the presence of someone special. She came from humble beginnings, raised by a single mother who worked multiple jobs to make ends meet, but Emily had made her first million by the age of 26, leading a team of over 150,000 entrepreneurs all over the world. She is a sought-after wellness teacher, speaker, and leading entrepreneur.

Few people work harder than Emily. She inspires millions of people through her business, podcast,[53] and social media. She is unapologetic, brave, and she seems to have it all. These days, she does.

Emily is who she is in part because she endured her own dark night of the soul, and I have watched her go through that with so much grace. Between interviews with A-list celebrities, she told me about the painful chapter in her life a few years ago, and how during that time, prayer sustained her and changed her life.

At that time, she told me she was separated from her then-husband. "We were just on two different wavelengths," she says, "and we had different priorities. I would pray over and over again, 'Make me fall in love with him. I don't want a divorce.' I had so much shame and guilt over it, trying to make it work, but I couldn't."

In fact, she refers to this period of her life as her "unanswered prayer." I asked her what happened then. What do we do when we ask, but the thing we pray for doesn't come?

"Well, first you've got to move your feet," she says. "I went to church, to the beach and the forest. Then, I had to sit with myself, and be honest with myself. When you sit still, you know the truth."

> "WHEN YOU SIT STILL, YOU KNOW THE TRUTH."

The truth didn't feel good. A fear of what others would think consumed Emily. Prayer offered the solace she needed; her faith carried through this time.

Emily says that in prayer, sometimes the message is very clear, but not always. Sometimes, she says, prayer is experimental; she might listen to a speaker, talk to a friend, or read a book, and see what she was drawn to, what pulled at her. "You just have to explore and let God reveal to you through art, through people, but most of all, through yourself, the benefit of suffering in those moments. And it's hard when you're in it because it's so freaking painful. And you're like, Why? Why? But it's building you. It's molding you."

---

53. Ford, E. (n.d.). *itsEmily*. [Podcast]. https://www.itsemily.com/podcast/

Even though Emily knew it would help her to be around other people, she simply didn't know how to ask for help; she believed she had to figure it out on her own. The people closest to her didn't understand what she was going through, and she felt utterly alone.

I remember taking a bath and just crying, uncontrollably sobbing. And I had a moment of wondering, would anyone even care if I wasn't here? Would anyone even care? And these things went through my head, like, is this how Kate Spade killed herself? I couldn't even believe I was going there. I thought, "Oh my God, has it come to this?" I just felt so much pain. I felt so alone. I didn't know how to operate alone; I was having issues with food. It was this storm of *What's next? What do you do?*

And it was this moment of desperation, of crying, of surrender [that] I surrendered.

And I was like, what do you want me to do with my life? Who do you want me to be? How do I come back from this? It was in that dark, painful moment that I just felt like a warm blanket came over me. I remember laying on my bathroom floor naked, just crying and crying and crying. And I heard this whisper in my ear that said, *Come back. Come back to me. Come back to me.* And I'm like, okay, how are we going to do this? Step by step, day by day. Step by step, day by day.

So, Emily took it day by day. She started saying yes to gatherings, going to church, and reading the Bible. She started to move her feet. It was that moment on the bathroom floor when she felt enveloped by the presence of love, that is, the result of her own intense prayer, which shifted her life.

Emily asked for help. She surrendered and trusted. And I am so grateful that she did. Emily reminds us that every obstacle we encounter on our path is a gift.

Emily says,

Prayer gave me the belief that this life is not about me. This life is about loving people and showing them how good it can be, how good it can really be, to know that they are loved—that

> "**PRAYER GAVE ME THE BELIEF THAT THIS LIFE IS NOT ABOUT ME**"

they can love and that they are loved. At the end of the day, you strip away all the stupid Gucci bags, you strip away this house and that trip and this stupid Instagram—at the end of the day, love is what makes life worth living. That's what we're all in the pursuit of. And it's right in front of us. It's already here. We just have to access it. That's it.

One of the things we do too rarely in our society is share moments like the one Emily shared. However, we will all undoubtedly have our own dark nights of the soul. Maybe we are in one even now.

We can ask for help. It's that easy. During our dark nights of the soul, we can surrender our disbelief and become open to receiving. These times in our lives can be transformative. Once we've survived the dark night and emerged into daylight again, we find we have become far more resilient and open to love.

You can download a guided prayer (audio and script) for surrender, along with other types of prayers, on my website under "prayers."[54]

Prayers of gratitude and love: Increasing vibration

The second way to use prayer effectively is simply to give thanks. Meister Eckhart wrote, "If the only prayer you say in your entire life is thank you, that would be sufficient." This form of directed intention,

---

54. www.jasnaburza.com/healerinheels

"THE MOST POWER-
FUL, NECESSARY
PRAYER OF ALL—
THE STRONG, DEEP,
SIMPLE THANK YOU"

which business mogul Bahram Akradi calls "the most powerful, necessary prayer of all—the strong, deep, simple thank you," is actually the fastest way to influence your energy field.

If you find yourself in a situation where you want to pray for something, instead of praying for what you want, pray for what is already there. Invoke the observer effect; activate the power of your focus and attention by directing that energy on the positive potentialities, which can then become reality. Give thanks for all the things that are working in your life and acknowledge their presence. If you practice gratitude daily, it will become a habit and you will experience more awe and wonder in your life. When this happens, we raise our vibration, become better able to access our higher self, and we open ourselves to the resonance that comes with aligning our actions with the sense of purpose that guides our lives.

The great thing about gratitude is that it gives us a sense of fulfillment. It also empowers us. Emily shared an example of such a prayer, saying,

> I woke up today and I'm like, "Thank you, God, for all this abundance. Thank you. I'm so excited for today. I'm going to create today. Who are you going to put in my path today? I'm excited. Let's make someone's day." I'm expressing gratitude, which puts me at a higher frequency, which is so beautiful. Praying for the day, thanking God for the day. That's typically how my prayer looks in the morning.

Here, Emily shows us what becomes possible when you tap into the power of prayer. In just a few words, she gives thanks for all that is, makes a request for guidance, expresses willingness to accept and greet whatever comes, and sets an intention for bringing all of this grace into the world.

Meditation as a form of prayer and transformation

Betsy Weiner, a meditation teacher and spiritual guide, is the type of a person who makes you feel like everything is going to be okay. She is a spiritual teacher as well, guiding many to find their true selves and live with grace, acceptance, and peace.

Betsy echoes so many things I discover in almost every conversation I have these days. She says, "People are faster to react to everything than ever before. There's no pause. There's no moment to just sit, to ask yourself the questions that need to be asked."

> "THERE'S NO MOMENT TO JUST SIT, TO ASK YOURSELF THE QUESTIONS THAT NEED TO BE ASKED."

Betsy notes that technology influences the pace of our lives; it is very difficult to resist the urge to be plugged in. She admits with a smile, "I would just say I'm as addicted to this thing in my hand as much as anybody else. I want to inhabit a world that looks pretty and has a filter on it." The problem arises when we remove ourselves from reality, wasting time and losing track of it affects us emotionally. She continues,

When I start comparing, I start feeling bad emotionally. Like, oh, I'm not doing enough. It's not polished enough. I should be doing more. Oh, I should be doing that. So that's where I get caught, in the belief that I am not doing enough. Then I start feeling bad and I go, oh, wait, I am feeling bad. Time to turn the phone off and do some earthing. Go put my feet on the grass and hug a tree.

Betsy wasn't always this peaceful and wise. She recounts a difficult story and a path to finding that peace.

"As a kid, I suffered. I ran as hard and as fast as I could from the discomfort." She was dealing with anorexia, she says, when she found yoga. "I was really suffering. I wanted to literally disappear. But I always had this thought: Maybe it's possible that I could not suffer so much and not experience so much pain. There has to be something bigger than me! I was looking for awe." She says she found that feeling of something bigger than her, that awe, when she would gaze at the stars.

For Betsy, yoga was a path to transformation. She emphasizes that there is no one prescription, no one way of coming out of the dark, the sense of being overwhelmed, or the pain. We have to find the path that fits us at this very moment.

She notes that it has to start with an awareness of the pain or sense of being overwhelmed. Emotions are at an all-time high; however, Betsy points out, "There's nothing rational about emotional thinking. It's emotional, which is fine. You can't fix an emotion. An emotion is like an arrow pointing in a direction to a thought or a belief. That's where you can do the work." When asked about formulas or quick fixes, she answers, "I used to be so much more prescriptive, but I have learned that you just have to start from here. Just start from this moment. What does this look like right now? Could you stop and just take a deep breath three times a day? Oh, yeah, I could do that. There you go. Let's start with that." The pressure to do all the things leaves us paralyzed with inaction and stuck in the same loop. Start small, she says, but utilize the emotions that point to what's really at stake.

For Betsy, there is one particular prayer from Jewish tradition called Modeh Ani ("I give thanks") that she adjusted to her liking. She says it changed her life. "I say a blessing every morning when I wake up: Thank you, God, for returning my soul to my body. Thank you for trusting me to be of service to the world today. Show me how

I can be of service today." It's a morning ritual that connects her to that sense of awe and affirms her deep desire to be of service.

Similar to anyone else, some days are harder than others, Betsy says, especially these current days. Betsy says,

> "THANK YOU, GOD, FOR RETURNING MY SOUL TO MY BODY. THANK YOU FOR TRUSTING ME TO BE OF SERVICE TO THE WORLD TODAY. SHOW ME HOW I CAN BE OF SERVICE TODAY."

> How do I bow in gratitude to pain and suffering? How do I do that? I have to practice. So, when something difficult happens—and difficult things have been happening lately—I bow and I say, okay, I am open to what this is going to teach me. Thank you. Thank you. I'm going to learn. And it's not easy at all, but it's either that or pushing it away and pretending like it's going to go away or trying to make it different or make it not hurt or feel bad, but at least I can step into it with that sense of removing my ego from it, as if it's about me in some way.

Part of surrendering is her meditation practice. Betsy says, "I think that meditation is practice for how to be that expression of the 'capital S' Self in the world. I feel like that's the practice field where I learn how to connect, learn how to move into the present moment, even in the midst of difficulty."

That is the task at hand and maybe the most difficult for these times: being present and allowing time to process and just be. To have the time to ask questions, be curious, and continue to search for something greater. The more I talk to people, the more I hear about a deep yearning for that occasional feeling that tells us we are not alone and that offers us solace and peace about today and the future. Betsy, with her smile that seems to hug me, reminds us that painful moments can be incredible opportunities for transformation—that we can all smile.

Blessing versus prayer

The older I get, the more I realize that many things my grandmothers did are being proven to work, even though we like to make fun of them in the modernized world. For example, blessing children and praying over them as well as blessing food. What does that do, if anything?

TO BLESS, IN ITS SIMPLEST FORM, IS TO WISH WELL UPON PEOPLE, OBJECTS, OR FOOD

Let's first talk about blessing versus prayer. To bless, in its simplest form, is to wish well upon people, objects, or food. To wish good things for someone or something is to state an intention that is specific and focused. Returning to the science behind the power of intention, we can clearly see reason to offer blessings—over meals, children, events, and more.

Dean Radin is the chief scientist at the Institute of Noetic Sciences and has published numerous books on consciousness. One in particular stood out to me, entitled *Real Magic*,[55] which is about the hidden power that resides within each individual. In this book, Radin describes a double-blind experiment conducted to learn whether beneficial intentions, such as, "a blessing, directed toward chocolate, would elevate the mood of people who ate it, more than the exact same chocolate that wasn't blessed."

The researchers crafted an intention that stated, "An individual who consumes this chocolate will manifest optimal health and functioning at physical, emotional and mental levels, and in particular will enjoy an increased sense of energy, vigor, and well-being." A group of Buddhist monks blessed the chocolate with this intention. The participants in the study were divided into three groups, two of which received chocolate that had been blessed, one of which was the control, which received chocolate that had not been blessed.

---

55. Radin, D. (2018). *Real Magic: Ancient Wisdom, Modern Science, and a Guide to the Secret Power of the Universe*. Harmony.

Radin wrote,

> What we found was that by the third day of eating chocolate, the average mood measure had improved more in the groups eating the blessed chocolate than in the control group, with odds against chance of 24 to 1. While this outcome is only modestly significant from a statistical perspective, it's suggested that based on the gold standard design for conducting a clinical test—a double blind, placebo control, randomized trial—the blessed chocolate altered subjective mood in a positive way.

Although this study may raise an eyebrow or two, the rigor of the study's protocol suggests that the strong results weren't a fluke. Just because something seems woo-woo doesn't mean it isn't true. I still remember when many people in the West considered acupuncture as woo-woo. Now that the benefits of this ancient tradition are widely known, that's changed. Why not with prayer?

A few years ago, I met Joey Korn, author of the book *Dowsing: A Path to Enlightenment.*[56] Decades of research suggested to Joey that humans and their emotions were creating something called discordant energies. Joey has been developing blessing processes for well over a decade in the belief that the blessed items will have different properties. Joey taught me a prayer that I now used to bless mine and my children's food every morning: "Please God, bless this food and charge it with energies so that you may bring healing to

"PLEASE GOD, BLESS THIS FOOD AND CHARGE IT WITH ENERGIES SO THAT YOU MAY BRING HEALING TO MY/OUR COMPLETE BEING, PHYS-ICALLY, MENTALLY, EMO-TIONALLY AND SPIRITUALLY. THANK YOU. AND SO IT IS."

---

56. Korn, J. (2004). *Dowsing: A Path to Enlightenment.* New Millennium Press.

my/our complete being, physically, mentally, emotionally and spiritually. Thank you. And so it is."

After studying the power of intention and being attuned to how our words and thoughts can in every way affect our lives, our surroundings, and the people around us, this little blessing has become not just a pleasant habit that makes me feel good, but a practice that I know has the power to fortify me, and it creates a positive energetic effect in the world. Why not try it? It costs nothing, it does no harm—and it may increase your wellbeing more than you think.

A prayer a day keeps the doctor away

Larry Dossey urges people to be inventive and creative in the ways they choose to pray. "No specific religion has a monopoly on prayer," he says.

> Be your own prayer master and concoct your own ceremonies. It comes down to love, caring, and compassion. It doesn't matter the words you use to describe prayer. Compassion, deep caring is the thing that bridges the gap between people… If people can focus on caring and compassion, it seems to liberate the forces that prayer relies on to help people get well.

What I love most about these findings regarding the benefits of prayer is that they validate and reinforce our elders' wisdom and they show us how we can easily implement various forms of prayer into our lives.

PRAYER IS AN ACT OF INTENTIONAL CONNECTION TO SOMETHING BIGGER THAN US AND BEING IN FULL SURRENDER OF AWE

Remember our definition here: Prayer is an act of intentional connection to something bigger than us and being in full surrender of awe. Regardless of your faith, praying can make your day go more smoothly, relieve stress, and benefit your physical and mental health. It also serves to reinforce our expectation of good in the world, which not only keeps you in a state of high vibration and opens you to resonance, it also activates the energetic potential for good to be realized in the world.

The specific language of our prayers and mantras are less important than the intention, emotion, and state of mind behind the act of prayer. Don't second guess yourself by needing to say the right words. All that matters is that you are sincere and honest about what you want. If you feel like repeating a mantra over and over again, do it! The more often we repeat a word or phrase, the more our brain begins to associate it with the state of being we want to cultivate.

Prayer can be an exercise in mindfulness in which you focus on the present moment and cultivate gratitude for what you have in your life. It can also be an opportunity to ask for guidance, reassurance, or help. It may take the form of meditation: Instead of focusing on your thoughts or emotions, you might allow the entire experience of prayer to wash over you like waves on a shore. A prayer practice requires only that you open your heart and mind to the universe. It allows you to connect with something greater than yourself, something that you believe in but cannot yet see or touch. Remember what Kierkegaard said: "Prayer does not change God, but it changes him who prays."

"PRAYER DOES NOT CHANGE GOD, BUT IT CHANGES HIM WHO PRAYS."

Exercise: Approaches to prayer

1. **Ask for help.** Whether this is a dark night of the soul in your life, think of something you are currently unable to handle on your own. Pray to be given the help you need.

2. **Give thanks.** Create prayers of gratitude and thanksgiving for the obvious blessings in your life; then for those things that you might grudgingly admit are blessings but that give you trouble; and then, give thanks for the current struggles in your life, opening yourself to the gifts these struggles will one day reveal.

3. **Pray for guidance.** Identify an area of your life that feels chaotic or directionless right now and pray for guidance. Ask for the clarity and coherence required to discern your next steps. The following is an example of a prayer I once heard and modified for my situation: "Dear God, (remember, even though I am not religious I use the word God but you can use Mother Nature, Source, Universe, the Great Unseen, etc.), where would you have me go? What would you have me do? How may I be of service to others? Please show me the sign and make it so obvious that I know it's from you. I believe."

4. **Bless indiscriminately.** Bless your food, your day, your loved ones, and people you don't love at all. Bless bad drivers, traffic, bad weather, bad hair days, badly behaved children, bad moods. Bless everything and everyone. Have fun with it—and see how quickly it lifts your spirits, raises your vibration, and restores your soul.

5. **Listen to recorded prayers.** Audio files of various recorded prayers are available for download on my website.[57]

---

57. www.jasnaburza.com/healerinheels

PART

III

THE GOD PARTICLE AND QUANTUM ENTANGLEMENT

One of the most enduring philosophical questions humans ask concerns our place in the universe. What is the relationship between the vastness of the cosmos and our little lives? Religion is going out of style in today's world, and with it, many of the most familiar stories about why we are here, how we should live, and whom we should serve. Nearly all of us ask ourselves, sooner or later, "What's the point of it all? Does life have meaning? What is my purpose? Why am I here?"

When we finally ask this question, it means we are ready to heed the call, to still the restlessness within, to listen to the answers that come, to fulfill our potential, and to move toward our highest good.

It has never been more important that we become aware of how we are all connected, bound together, and upheld by an invisible tapestry. This holds true even in the face of society's efforts to amplify our sense of disconnection, of separateness and alienation from ourselves, each other, and the universe as a whole.

Einstein said,

A human being is part of the whole called by us Universe… a part limited in time and space. He experiences his thoughts and feelings as separate from the rest—a kind of optical delusion of his own consciousness. This delusion is a prison for us, restricting us to our personal desires and to affection for a few persons nearest to us. Our task must be to free ourselves from this prison by widening our compassion to embrace all living creatures and the whole of nature and its beauty.[58]

In this final section of the book, I will introduce you to the "God's particle," the discovery of which won the Nobel Prize in physics, and which proves the existence of an energetic field connecting everything and everyone. As we learn about this intricately woven web of which we are a part, we begin to see the implications for our lives, our cultures, and our planet unfold. When we tap into that energetic interdependence and cosmic connection, we can not only heal one another and ourselves but also align ourselves with its infinite, resonant power, and awaken the genius within.

ALL OF US, AND I MEAN *ALL*, ARE CAPABLE OF FAR MORE THAN WE THINK WE ARE

All of us, and I mean *all*, are capable of far more than we think we are. The key to finding happiness, meaning, and wholeness lies in waking up to that potential and becoming aware of our purpose. We are so much more than a structure of muscle and bones that breathes, strives, worries, and accumulates nonsensical stuff along the way.

---

58. Einstein, A. (2005). Letter, February 12, 1950. In A. Calaprice, (Ed.). *The New Quotable Einstein*, p. 206. Princeton University Press.

When we get to the point of becoming whole, we become vessels of this universe. We are then utilized by something far greater than ourselves for the good of others and the world. Then, a funny thing happens—as we do this, we become fulfilled, happy, and whole. Because it is in giving that we receive. We realize that the ultimate goal is to tap our potential, and then give it away. We do that through the things we are most suited for: writing, painting, teaching, building, designing.

Quantum mechanics demonstrates the interconnectedness of all things, and it can give us clues as we learn to access the genius within. This is not about following the edict of some unreachable deity; it's about realizing that, as Jesus is said to have said, "these and far greater things we shall do," because we—just as we are—are the ones we have been waiting for.

When we break down the atom, we enter the subatomic world of quarks. Go further, and when we break those down, we arrive at the foundational building blocks of which all else is made: particles whose behavior is still so mysterious we have no word for them but "God." Beyond that, matter is no longer divisible; reduce a particle any further and it shifts form, becoming a wave of energy. At our core, that inchoate swirl of energy is all we are.

10

The Quantum Mechanics of Love: Activating the "God Particle" for Good

Everyone thinks of changing the world, but no one thinks of changing himself.

—Leo Tolstoy

The soldiers stormed into our house like they owned it. They wore uniforms and had guns. Most of them were young—boys I had seen around town—but now their voices were deeper, and they spoke with authority.

"Take off your damn shoes," I snapped. It was the only thing that gave me power. I knew I couldn't prevent them from coming into my house, but they could take off their damn shoes, as was custom. What, have we lost manners now?

For a moment, I'd forgotten this was war.

They had come for my dad. These boys were going around town with their guns, rounding up Moslem men between the ages of 16 and 64. My dad was a proclaimed atheist, but he had married a Moslem woman: guilty enough.

"Where is Mr. Burza?"

"I don't know," was Mama's reply. We all knew better.

"Do you know you're lying to the authorities?"

"I am not lying, sir," Mama said to a boy to whom she could have given birth twice.

"We'll be back," he said, and they all turned around.

"And… and take off your damn shoes!" I yelled. One of them turned around and gave me the look.

Mama pushed me aside. "Go… go. She is just a little girl and doesn't know what she is saying."

However, I did. I wanted a reaction. I wanted them to get angry, to show their real faces. I wanted them to hit me so I could feel something. Yes, we were being bombed, and, yes, this was war, but why did I feel such pain and confusion when I wasn't even hurt, as many true war victims are?

They kept coming back, and my dad kept hiding. He was the only adult man in the neighborhood who wasn't taken away. Instead of being thankful the soldiers didn't take everyone, the neighborhood housewives became upset their husbands were being tortured while my dad was still hiding. They began to say he wasn't a true man. Something happens to people under duress: they want everyone to suffer. As if that will ease their pain.

I was playing in my aunt's front yard next door when I saw it: my father, his hands behind his back, unsteady on his feet, was being dragged away by those boys. They were heading toward a blue van that had bars on the windows. I remember it in slow motion. I stood, frozen, ready to test the soldiers' limits, to say a swear word—something! But my dad knew me, and he knew I had his temper. "You should have been a boy," he used to say.

My father communicated something to me with his eyes, and I held my tongue. For us children, one look from our dad, a raised eyebrow, was enough to make us stop.

This was a different look, though. I stood there not knowing what to do. The look said, "Don't you dare move" and "It's ok" at the same time.

The boys shoved him into the van and pulled away.

I grew up watching people do inconceivable things to one another—inflict violence, torture, rape—in the name of faith. I vowed to be different: more accepting, more loving, and more understanding. I made my way to the United States, a bastion of freedom, a place where it didn't matter where you came from, what your political or religious background was—a place for me, I thought. For many years, it was. However, the past few years have given us reason to doubt each other and ourselves. We fixate on our differences, doubling down on our beliefs. Emotions are high, people are pulling apart, division is being systematically sown. The longer it goes on, the more it becomes the norm. We often partake in foolish conflicts, picking sides and getting sucked into the rush of a story that races forward, a story we're not even sure is true.

This is not a disquisition on politics or morality, or an effort to claim territory, stake out right and wrong. I will leave that work for the next messiah. However, I do believe that by taking a clear look at ourselves and our participation in the chaos of the present world, we can take steps to change the nature of the influence we have, stop inflicting and incurring injuries and harm, and instead direct our energy toward the healing we—all of us—desperately need.

The "God particle"

We have all heard stories about twins being unusually connected, to the extent of sharing a private language, sensing each other's thoughts or state of mind even when separated, and feeling each other's physical pain. We may have had one of those coincidences where just as we're thinking about someone, they call us on the phone. Until recently, science didn't have an explanation for phenomena such as these; often enough, they told us we were imagining things.

However, in 2012, when the Nobel Prize in physics went to the team that discovered the Higgs boson particle—colloquially known as the God particle—the smallest, most elementary particle in the known universe was suddenly very big news.

Think of particles as building blocks. Everything that exists—energy, matter, and every shape matter can take—consists of these building blocks. Take the human body: At the end of the day, it's just a big collection of cells. Even if you break the body down into its many constituent cells, those cells can be broken down again into the building blocks of which they're made: atoms. Atoms, too, are made up of something even smaller: When we break down the atom, we enter the subatomic world of quarks. Go further, and when we break those down, we arrive at the foundational building blocks of which all else is made: particles whose behavior is still so mysterious we have no word for them but "God." Beyond that, matter is no longer divisible; reduce a particle any further and it shifts form, becoming a wave of energy. At our core, that inchoate swirl of energy is all we are.

PARTICLES WHOSE BEHAVIOR IS STILL SO MYSTERIOUS WE HAVE NO WORD FOR THEM BUT "GOD." BEYOND THAT, MATTER IS NO LONGER DIVISIBLE; REDUCE A PARTICLE ANY FURTHER AND IT SHIFTS FORM, BECOMING A WAVE OF ENERGY. AT OUR CORE, THAT INCHOATE SWIRL OF ENERGY IS ALL WE ARE.

Now, let me introduce you to the Higgs field: the unseen quantum field discovered at CERN, the European Organization for Nuclear Research in Switzerland, home to the Hadron Collider. It's the world's largest and most complex scientific instrument used to study fundamental particles. This quantum field contains everything that exists; it is within us and all around us. It binds those waves of energy, turning them into fundamental particles. This force is what turns us from energy to matter; it's the reason you and I are not fairy dust.

This is the true cosmic tapestry—intricately woven, elegantly designed. In classical (Newtonian) physics, most systems can be observed and measured. Not quantum physics. We are learning that the true nature of reality does not observe deterministic or fixed scientific laws for this reason: Human behavior—our thoughts, our actions, human consciousness—interacts with the subatomic world in a way that we have yet to explain fully.

I cannot help but be reminded of what the Sufi poet Rumi wrote: "Out beyond ideas of wrongdoing and rightdoing, there is a Field. I will meet you there."

Spooky action at a distance

In 1935, Albert Einstein and his colleagues discovered something they called quantum entanglement: When atoms come into contact with one another, they create a bond, which can be observed no matter how far apart these atoms are. They can communicate, and their behavior continues to share a mutual influence, no matter how far they grow apart. In other words, if two entangled particles become physically separated, they continue

IF TWO ENTANGLED PARTICLES BECOME PHYSICALLY SEPARATED, THEY CONTINUE TO BEHAVE AS IF THEY ARE STILL PHYSICALLY TOGETHER, A PHENOMENON REFERRED TO AS *NON-LOCALITY* to behave as if they are still physically together, a phenomenon referred to as *non-locality*. One particle knows what the other one is doing; in this regard, they share the same "state." All of this is based on the principle of *superposition*, a term that describes how particles, like waves, can be in many places at once, and can affect one another's state. The principle of entanglement applies to space as well as time, meaning that changes in the state of current particles affect the entangled pair in the past and even the future.

Einstein thought he was wrong; he died having ascribed his results to an error. In a famous paper published in 1935 called the "EPR Paradox," Einstein and two of his colleagues, Boris Podolsky and Nathan Rosen, concluded that quantum theory was not an adequate description of the atomic and subatomic world.

In October 2022, Alain Aspect, John F. Clauser, and Anton Zeilinger received the Nobel Prize in Physics for their work using entangled photons to test the quantum foundations of reality. Their experiments proved that quantum entanglement is real, and Einstein and his colleagues were wrong.

Lee Billings, reporting on the 2022 Nobel Laureates in Physics for *Scientific American*,[59] wrote,

> Working independently, each of the three researchers forged new experiments demonstrating and investigating quantum entanglement, the curious phenomenon in which two or more particles exist in a so-called entangled state. In this bizarre situation, an action taken on one of the particles can instantaneously ripple through the entire entangled assemblage, predicting the other particles' behavior, even if they are far apart. If an observer determines the state of one such

---

59. Billings, L. (2022, October 4). Explorers of quantum entanglement win 2022 Nobel Prize in Physics. *Scientific American.* https://www.scientificamerican.com/article/explorers-of-quantum-entanglement-win-2022-nobel-prize-in-physics1/

particle, its entangled counterparts will instantly reflect that state—whether they are in the same room as the observer or in a galaxy on the opposite side of the universe. Although this phenomenon has become an essential aspect of modern quantum technologies, it is so counterintuitive and seemingly impossible that Albert Einstein once famously derided it as "spooky action at a distance."

If you're a bit confused by now, good. This is part of awakening our access to genius: an understanding of the foundations of life can change the way we perceive, move through, and ultimately affect the world. For our purposes, becoming aware of how interconnectedness and entanglement work at the particle level can illuminate the way in which our emotional states affect others and theirs affect us. Now more than ever, we must learn to love our neighbors. We must become a vibrational match for concordance rather than discord, resonance rather than dissonance, joy rather than pain.

WE MUST BECOME A VIBRATIONAL MATCH FOR CONCORDANCE RATHER THAN DISCORD, RESONANCE RATHER THAN DISSONANCE, JOY RATHER THAN PAIN

When we emotionally become attached to someone, positively or negatively, something happens: similar to particles, we become entangled. Changes in our state affect the other person, and the other way around. Say you had a bad falling out with someone. They hold a grudge and so do you. Them thinking of you while negatively charged affects you no matter how far away you are. Likewise, their willingness to heal themselves, forgive you, and send you love will also affect you; so will your healing efforts affect them.

When we heal, forgive, and emanate love, we allow others to do the same. We activate this power every time we meditate, every time we laugh and let go of hurt. To recognize our participation in today's social conflict is to claim responsibility for the thoughts and actions we put into the world. By changing the way in which we move in the world, we change the world.

I don't forget. However, I forgive

Albert Einstein said that the most important question we can ask is whether we live in a friendly or hostile universe. The quality of our lives depends on the way in which we answer that question. Not only that, I believe we are here to make the world better for us and everyone else through not just actions but also thoughts and emotions.

In 2020, I lost many close friends who I viewed as family; I stopped being invited to family events because of my beliefs. I vehemently disagreed with certain beliefs they held, but I never considered not loving them or refusing to have a civilized conversation. Often, when political or ideological issues arise, we feel we have to take a stand. However, I have never seen the level of alienation I see arising today from differing beliefs.

So many cultural forces encourage us to see how separate we are. To divide and conquer. To separate and engulf. If physics and mystics alike tell us we are all a part of the same cosmic tapestry, who are we to separate ourselves—and from what, from whom? The more we accentuate and affirm our separateness, the more we cultivate a culture of loneliness, isolation, and despair.

THE MORE WE ACCENTUATE AND AFFIRM OUR SEPARATENESS, THE MORE WE CULTIVATE A CULTURE OF LONELINESS, ISOLATION, AND DESPAIR

How do we love others regardless of their beliefs? Okay, love may be taking it too far. Then how do we at least respect and recognize the divine spark in everyone we meet? I asked Mark Dayton, the former Governor of Minnesota, this very question.

"To love is tough, I think," he says. "To me, it's about respecting the humanity of another person, the shared humanity we have."

Mark worked in the political sphere for more than 40 years. I asked him how, in that most mentally, emotionally, and perhaps morally brutal of professions, he could maintain his sense of ethics, purpose, and peace. He told me he had to align himself with the God within, seeking guidance and coherence from that source so he could be of service to others.

Mark also received guidance from his colleague and friend Ted Kennedy. Ted invited Mark to visit him at his family home in Maine. As the two men walked along the beach, Ted gave Mark a few words of advice.

"He said that perseverance is the prerequisite for success in politics," Mark recalls. "It doesn't guarantee success, but it's a prerequisite. You have to persevere in the face of failure and backlash. Persevere through the failings and the ridicule. You have to tune that out. You have to ignore it."

Compassion

When I was 15, I started dating Peter. Peter wasn't Moslem. I liked him anyway. I knew my father wouldn't approve, so one day I asked him what he thought. I will never forget that day.

He told me what had happened: the beatings, sleeping in the elementary school gym, watching young boys being beaten in front of him when he couldn't do anything to stop it. He spoke of being on the front lines of battle and thinking that every minute would be his last. I imagined the trenches and how cold he must have been; I knew he didn't like to be cold. I also imagined they must have forced him to do things he didn't want to do.

I screamed, "I hate them. I hate them all," but he remained calm. He told me that most of the guards were boys who didn't know what they were doing.

"Honey, would you have taken up a gun three years ago to fight?" he asked.

"Yes!" I screamed. "YES!"

"See, such a nice girl was ready to hurt someone. Is that who you are?"

"No." I couldn't believe what I was saying.

"Most of these boys just did what they were told because they didn't have any other choice, or because they were afraid. People aren't inherently bad; they just act as such sometimes. Forgive them, for they didn't know what they were doing."

> **I AM CAPABLE OF MURDER; SO ARE YOU. AS HUMANS, WE HAVE THE PREDISPOSITION BOTH TO BE GOOD AND TO DO GREAT HARM.**

I am capable of murder; so are you. As humans, we have the predisposition both to be good and to do great harm. The history books are replete with evidence of the human desire for control and the willingness to manipulate, steal, hurt, and kill. Even in our contemporary world, these traits are visible everywhere, division sown and deepened by ideology and conformity. I know all too well where these trends lead, having grown up in a country torn by war, split along the fault lines of three ethnicities. Being born into an ethnicity and a family of certain beliefs forced me into a refugee camp. *But Jasna*, I hear people say, *that would never happen here in the U.S.* It has in the past, and it could again. We could turn this around; we could do the work to learn from where we are, to let it teach us, to let it lead us back to compassion, freedom, and peace.

We have to start to take responsibility that we are also somehow part of the concerning trends that we complain about over coffee with our friends. Our almost habitual knee-jerk reactions, our judgment of others, and our dismissal of the value of their views is a way to inflict pain. Hurt people hurt people. Every time we are triggered and react with hate or judgment, we lose a part of ourselves. That is not who we are.

These individuals can become our teachers. Whether you are troubled by a political figure, spouse, co-worker, or neighbor, they can provide a mirror of sort, allowing you a glimpse into the dark nooks and crannies of who and where you are. What part of me is reacting and why? Why am I being aggressive? What's causing me to lose my footing in this situation? Where does this reaction come from? Although this is difficult when we see ourselves as separate, setting ourselves up in a self-righteous conflict of us against them, we need to remember that hatred is nothing but self-inflicted pain. We are all one.

Our "great secret weapon"

Even as love sometimes eludes us or becomes lost in life's busy shuffle, we all know the power of love. Now, research has given us the data we need to understand the science behind what we already suspect: Love is the most powerful force in the universe.

"The power of love to change bodies is legendary," writes Larry Dossey, "built into folklore, common sense, and everyday experience. Love moves the flesh; it pushes matter around—as the blushing and palpitations experienced by lovers attest. Throughout history, 'tender, loving care' has uniformly been recognized as a valuable element in healing."[60]

Gloria Prema[61] writes, "It has been found that the heart generates over 50,000 femtoteslas (a measure of electromagnetic fields, or EMFs) compared to less than 10 femtoteslas generated by the brain.

---

60. Dossey, L. (1995). *Healing Words: The Power of Prayer and the Practice of Medicine*. HarperOne

61. Prema, G. (2022). *It's All Light: Juicy Science Meets Spirituality Without Religion*. Independently Published.

"HEART'S ELECTROMAG-NETIC FIELD IS 5,000 TIMES MORE POWERFUL THAN THE BRAIN'S ELEC-TROMAGNETIC FIELD."

So we can see that the heart's electromagnetic field is 5,000 times more powerful than the brain's electromagnetic field."

Steve used to tell me that love comes from the spiritual realm, and as such, it is an energizing, coherent, creative entity that makes it more powerful—and more persuasive—than other types of emotion and information. When we are aligned and engaged through our intention with love, it manifests in our physical world and helps us create coherence in the body. Love has occupied the minds of prophets, mystics, and poets throughout the ages. As Rumi wrote, "I looked in temples, churches, and mosques. But I found the Divine within my heart."

Love has the highest frequency and power for change. It helps us remove the illusion of separation from others. If we know there is no separation, we can act on the knowledge that we are connected to everything else in the universe, and we take responsibility for the power of our thoughts, feelings, and actions to affect the lives of other people and the larger world.

Our heart is not just an organ; it's an electromagnetic device that, in addition to its everyday function of pumping blood, emanates energy, creating a field around us that devices and other people can measure and feel. The heart holds the key to connection at both a physical and emotional level; it has the power we need to connect with our higher selves, resonate with others, and heal.

Research conducted at the HeartMath Institute reveals this: "The heart is the most powerful source of electromagnetic energy in the human body, producing the largest rhythmic electromagnetic field of any of the body's organs."[62] Not only can medical devices measure this energy and tests such as the EKG and the ECG interpret the

---

62. HeartMath Institute. (n.d.). Science of the heart: Exploring the role of the heart in human performance. https://www.heartmath.org/research/science-of-the-heart/energetic-communication/

data; other people can feel it. The heart's electromagnetic field extends several feet from the body, and our emotions and thoughts affect its energy's tone.

If our heart is in a state of coherence, which we can affect by tuning out the noise, recon-

"THE HEART IS THE MOST POWERFUL SOURCE OF ELECTROMAGNETIC ENERGY IN THE HUMAN BODY, PRODUCING THE LARGEST RHYTHMIC ELECTROMAGNETIC FIELD OF ANY OF THE BODY'S ORGANS"

textualizing our perceptions, and intentionally directing our energy in positive ways—we emanate that coherence. That's why some people are so calming to be around; we are attuned to and positively affected by their highly coherent heart state. The same can be said of those who are in a state of incoherence—they emanate chaotic heart energy and create feelings of discomfort in others. Because we all affect each other energetically, it is vital to become more aware of our own energetic states and their effects.

Of all the ways to create coherence, reach resonance, and increase conscious awareness in others and ourselves, heart coherence is the most powerful. The feeling of love naturally draws us into a state of greater coherence and alignment. Gloria Prema writes, "Through love and compassion we grow in evolutionary terms. This has been lost to a world which is obsessed with technological fixes, which values the intellect above love and compassion. Every spiritual tradition teaches that love and compassion are the number one law: spiritual healing practised [throughout the world] is an ancient practice and it works by transmitting love, seen as light, which enables a person to come into a state of coherence and in our own lives we know that love and compassion heal us."

Can love fail?

Who hasn't had a relationship turn sour? It's important to note that sometimes it's healthy and necessary to move on and remove negative people from our life. We still owe it to ourselves to clean the energy and clear out the toxic cobwebs of those relationships. Those breaks sometimes leave negative energy that, if unresolved, can wreak havoc on our physical and mental health. The following are three tips for transforming those negative relationships we actually want to keep.

1. Very often, a break in a relationship is due to miscommunication or actual or perceived hurt. In this situation, write a letter of forgiveness and love. Taking responsibility for our actions. Showing forgiveness transforms the energy between people. Write about them in a positive way and focus only on the good because in the end, we are all one. This practice heals you as well.

2. Do something kind for the other person. This really works: If you have a tenuous relationship with someone, it's easy to get angry or resentful. Break the tension by going out of your way to do something kind and thoughtful for them. When we do this, we not only feel better ourselves, we shift the energy in the relationship with that person in our mind.

3. Other people are often our mirror; there *is* a reason they are in our lives. By meditating and focusing on our inner experience, we energetically change our vibration, thoughts, and feelings, and thus, alter the tone of this entanglement; the other person is bound to feel the energetic shift as well.

You have to give what you want to receive

LOVE IS A BOOMERANG Love is a boomerang. Even when we don't receive love from those to whom we offer it, its energetic power returns to us even in ways we don't see. I was reminded of this when I spoke with entrepreneur Dario Otero. In the community where he grew up, he said there was the common concept of the "circulating dollar."

"When you don't have a lot of money," Dario told me, "and then you get a little bit of money, you tend to circulate it within your community, because when you don't have the money again, somebody will take care of you.

"That was love," he continued. "Love is like this currency that's just circulating. It works, once you give it out."

When we love, it changes our vibration and our resonance; it's only natural that we will be loved back and taken care of, no matter what. Love creates an energy field that brings coherence, alignment, and goodness into our lives.

Exercise: Practice forgiveness and break the negatively charged entanglement

Think of someone you have hurt or who has hurt you. Forgive yourself and forgive them. Write it out. Say it out loud. Pray for their wellbeing and for everyone who was ever engaged in that relationship. Release the need to be right. Remember this doesn't mean you have to let them into your life or approve of their actions. It's likely you will have a very powerful emotional reaction by doing that, you may even end up crying. That is how you learn to love yourself. It is how you learn to love who you are becoming. Let them go. Withhold judgment. As you do, think of these words by Omar Khayyam:

"If you're not a drinker;
do not cut down those who do,
Don't start politics and deceit.
Don't be so proud of the fact
that you don't drink,
You probably take hundreds of bites
that may be worse than drinking."[63]

---

63. Akradi, B. (n.d.). Working with others. https://bahramakradi.com/working-with-others

We become vessels for something great, and we come to under-stand the symphony of life. We know why we do what we do, and we have a sense of inner peace very few come to know.

CHAPTER 11

Purpose: Life Is Work Versus Life's Work

The two most important days in your life are the day you were born and the day you find out why.

—Mark Twain

That fourth miscarriage hit me hard. Becoming a mother was almost a side gig, a secondary interest I pursued while keeping most of my focus on becoming the most successful person I knew. Plowing through life with sheer immigrant determination and grit, I was going to make it all work. Somehow.

All along, there were signs that something was off, that I was not on my true path—but I didn't want to admit that. When we're ignoring the signs, we risk being hit hard with something that will really get our attention. That fourth miscarriage did it; I was at a turning point. The doctor told me I would likely never have children; the doctor also asked me if I was happy and whether things were going ok at work. That made me pause. What did that have to do with it? Everything.

Meaning is crucial to human life. In his book *Man's Search for Meaning*,[64] Viktor Frankl echoed Friedrich Nietzsche by relating that he who has a *why* to live can bear with almost any *how*. Having purpose means having a clear why—a reason for doing what we do. Without that sense of purpose and meaning, we may find ourselves plagued by uncertainty about who we are and what we're doing here.

I found my sense of purpose through pain, anxiety, and a deep sense of loss. No, I didn't welcome it or love it at the time. But it had something to teach me.

At the time, I slept with my phone (a Blackberry, back then) under my pillow so that I wouldn't miss any important messages in the middle of the night. I wasn't happy, content, or fulfilled. I didn't even remember what those things were. Even closing a big deal provided nothing more than a temporary high that was invariably followed by a crash into numbness and emptiness. I was on my fourth miscarriage and still trying to maintain the façade of success and achievement that I felt was expected, even required, of me—but by whom? I couldn't answer that. All I knew was that I felt immense pressure to be someone important. In reality, I was living someone else's life.

IN REALITY, I WAS LIVING SOMEONE ELSE'S LIFE

Doctor's questions gave me pause. In that pause, I started to ask my own questions. Thus began my journey of discovery, one of the greatest gifts of my life. It gave me the space to create meaning and purpose. It was a process; I went on to have five more miscarriages. However, I was becoming more aligned with who I was each day, and every small improvement gave me more energy to move forward.

Ultimately, I made the radical changes that gave my life purpose. I had two beautiful children in one year. I am so grateful for them as

---

64. Frankl, V. (2006). *Man's Search for Meaning*. Beacon Press.

well as for a new lease on life. Pain was the instigator; it gave me a moment to pause and reflect. First, it forced me and then it inspired me to be more mindful and specific about who I am, what I want, and who I intend to become.

Numerous recent studies found that a subjective sense of having meaning or purpose in life associates with better health outcomes. In addition to measurable health markers such as lower blood pressure and lower rates of depression and anxiety, people who report a sense of meaning or purpose were more likely to say they were satisfied with their lives as a whole. Purpose is not like kale, which is beneficial and helpful for *some* people; purpose is helpful for us *all*.

When we become aligned with the reason we're here, there is a sense of peacefulness, surrender, and acceptance. We become better equipped to address whatever comes our way. When our lives are purposeful, we proceed from the belief that everything in it serves a purpose as well. Purpose is an anchor, a rudder, a compass; it gives us the assurance that we can continue on our path no matter who or what tries to throw us off.

> **PURPOSE IS NOT LIKE KALE, WHICH IS BENEFICIAL AND HELPFUL FOR *SOME* PEOPLE; PURPOSE IS HELPFUL FOR US *ALL***

Michelle Henry was set to open her first franchise of Face Foundrié[65] right before the pandemic hit—and then everything came to a halt. Any business owner who has invested huge amounts of time and money in a new venture knows the anxiety and pain of that experience. However, Michelle had something deeper that guided her. I asked her how she kept her faith and she told me about her pull toward purpose but also how she was first getting herself into resonance and alignment. She says,

> A lot of it was really focusing inward on manifesting. I would go on this kind of meditative walk. I was really trying to see

---

65. Henry, M. (n.d.). *Face Foundrié.* www.facefoundrie.com/about

the positive and what I wanted out of a certain situation. I would walk five or six miles a day. It was such a heavy time. I would always start my walks by thinking about what I was grateful for. What was the little tiny light? What was the positive moment? And it could be something so small. I got a free coffee, or I was able to see my kids complete an activity—really tiny things that I could really place gratitude on. That was something that was really important to me. Write it down by hand, don't be afraid to write down how you feel in the moment and ultimately what you want in the future because it's okay to feel sad, it's okay to be down. I mean, I feel like there's got to be a realistic measure. The last three years have been completely wild and traumatic, and people need to own that and own their experiences. And I find that it's nice to journal and write things down, but ultimately, I always try to end it with: What do I want to see in the future? It might be sticky right now, it might not be easy right now, but what is my goal? Are there easy ways to get out of this or maneuver? And nine times out of ten, the answer is probably no.

A solution, she says, will come to you eventually if you keep fixating on it.

Michelle may seem like an overnight success to so many, but her success is a result of alignment with her calling and the work she put into her dreams. There is often glamour associated with a sense of purpose and those who have found it, but the process of getting there is often sticky. It's often filled with hard **THE PATH WILL UNFOLD IF YOU KEEP WALKING** work and disappointment, but the path will unfold if you keep walking. More important, it's about who you become in the process.

She tells me a story, one that's common and that Michelle says she wishes she heard more.

I was broke when I started a few businesses. I was bartending. I had a screen-printing machine. I was trying to make ends meet doing odd jobs. I was biking to save gas money. I never shy away from reflecting on some of those hard times. And what really gives me comfort is that if I ever had to go back to those hard times, I've already lived through it. I got this. So, if I had to go back and bike, I can do that. I'm fine with that. Do I like fancy things and finer things? Yeah, there's always a nice appreciation for that. But I've lived both, and it doesn't scare me on that flip side because I've already lived it.

On work

In my profession, it is a common occurrence to see courses for passive income with an emphasis of "never work again," and their focus is on riches and fame. I love money and abundance and the freedom I believe we should all have. However, as these modern business/abundance gurus prey upon our unmanifested desires, they fail to teach us one thing: Our work is holy.

In the words of Gary Zukav, "When the personality comes fully to serve the energy of the soul, that is authentic power." When we find that something for which we are aligned, it is as if the entire universe comes together. Too often, we follow societal instructions for work of what is acceptable or safe. Few of us commit to our true passions, and who can blame us? However, our true work is life-giving; it is an expression of life.

> "WHEN THE PERSONALITY COMES FULLY TO SERVE THE ENERGY OF THE SOUL, THAT IS AUTHENTIC POWER."

This reminds me of the words from the most beautiful poem by Khalil Gibran:

Always you have been told that work is a curse and labour a misfortune.

But I say to you that when you work you fulfill a part of earth's furthest dream, assigned to you when that dream was born,

And in keeping yourself with labour you are in truth loving life,

And to love life through labour is to be intimate with life's inmost secret.

Work is love made visible.

And if you cannot work with love but only with distaste, it is better that you should leave your work and sit at the gate of the temple and take alms of those who work with joy.[66]

You will find that some of the most meaningful and profound moments in life occur when we do something in the service of others. These are moments when we are being used by the force that created us to create something or to improve something. To access these moments, you have to trust yourself and pay attention to where you are feeling the pull. Instead of others dictating your purpose, you must trust your own voice.

Former Governor of Minnesota, Mark Dayton, is a prime example of someone who had the clarity he needed to know his purpose and chart a course according to that knowledge, with or without support or approval, no matter what obstacles he faced. In politics, he says,

You have to persevere in the face of failure. I stopped reading comments a long time ago. You have to tune that out. I ignore it; I'm human like anybody, but it just comes with the territory. And if I believe I'm right, then if I think I'm wrong or if I

---

66. Gibran, K. (2019). *The Prophet*. Penguin.

made a mistake—then it hurts. This one comes with the territory. This reminds me of a Harry Truman quote: "If you can't
stand the heat, get out of the kitchen." There's also the saying
that if you want a friend in Washington, get a dog."

"It's hard sometimes when you see politics bring out the best in
people, and also bring out the worst," Mark adds. "I see the baser
motives of people." Even in the political sphere, he says, agreeing
upon a political philosophy of nonviolence, "is maybe the first step
towards loving. If you can't love somebody, at least don't be violent
towards them. But then you're really going against the grain because
the human psyche is so ingrained with this allowance and human-
ization of anybody who looks different or disagrees."

I asked Mark what helps him keep clarity, or, when he has lost
that, to find it again.

He says,

I tried to do meditation for 50 years, unsuccessfully. I have a
monkey mind. When I need to make important decisions, I
get out of my knees at night before going to sleep and pray for
divine wisdom. And sometimes I feel like I get it, sometimes
I don't. But I often get a sense of guidance. I have a system
where I ask myself or I ask my atman, my God within, for
guidance.

Mark's sense of purpose and his dedication to the cause of the greater
public good haven't protected him from either the slings and errors
or public life or the suffering that comes to every human being in the
form of heartache, loneliness, and love.

"I went through one of my dark nights of the soul. I was in
despair for six months and was hoping for something to hold on to.
I had a relationship that ended. I got dumped, I was very much in
love. It was very painful." That breakup came a few years after Mark's

195

divorce. Mark, who's been sober since 1987, realized that being sober meant,

> I had no buffer. I went to this refuge about an hour west of Minneapolis, run by this Christian couple. I was in a little shack by myself. I signed up for three days and for two days was literally going crazy. There's no diversion. It was August. And I just asked questions about something and then asked to be given a sign. I wanted to see number 12 as a confirmation. I always thought 12 was a mystical number.

That sign came to Mark in a vivid dream. "I was so clear and it's like, wow, this work is worth something here." He continues,

> I started doing some spiritual reading. I was a special student for a year at United Theological Seminary to study Christian ethics—and say, anybody who has been in politics could use a refresher course on Christian ethics. But I did a lot of reading about Bahai, Sufi, and the mystical traditions. Somebody said religion is for people who are afraid of going to hell, and spirituality is for people who've been to hell in order to try to get back. And here I was in hell, trying to work my way back.
>
> **"RELIGION IS FOR PEOPLE WHO ARE AFRAID OF GOING TO HELL, AND SPIRITUALITY IS FOR PEOPLE WHO'VE BEEN TO HELL"**
>
> I had two German shepherds with me the whole time. There was a study a few years ago that if you pet a dog, your physiology changes. Your brain waves turn to positivity, your relaxation increases significantly. I read this, I thought, well, try to come home. Everybody in the world hates me. My two shepherds are wagging their tails and I just want to be conscious of just getting down on the floor and petting them. And sure enough, within a minute I

was feeling more relaxed and more positive. They were a huge ally in surviving the turmoil of my pursuits.

I asked Mark what advice he gives people who are facing their own dark nights of the soul. He says,

Well, when you're going through hell, keep on going. Part of it, again, is that you trust. You just have to put one foot in front of the other and keep on walking through it and believe that at some point this too shall pass. I think you have to do psychological repair. I think you have to do psychotherapy in some way that connects you with what's going on right then because there's something deeper inside of it. If it's a really dark night, there's something deeper that's part of that. You've fallen into a hole, but it becomes a pit because of what underlies it. So, I think you have to do the psychological work to understand and hopefully clean it out. You got to bring that puss up. It's horrible. There's an opportunity to completely reshape. If you just stuff it down and keep on blowing up at your kids or your spouse or whoever, you're not going to remedy it or move beyond it. And I think you have to find a spiritual beacon—God, or whoever, whatever.

> **"WELL, WHEN YOU'RE GOING THROUGH HELL, KEEP ON GOING"**

Mark has absolute clarity on his own purpose in life, which is simply this:

Trying to make the world a better place. That's right. But it's true. Try to advance personal freedom and opportunity. The Declaration of Independence says, "hold these truths to be self-evident: that all men and women are created equal." They're endowed by their Creator with certain unalienable rights: life, liberty, and the pursuit of happiness. The right to be alive and free of poverty and oppression. Liberty, the freedom to the right to make your own decisions in life as long as they're moral and within the bounds of reason. Not to have somebody else dictating what you can or cannot do. And the pursuit of happiness. We're all striving to find personal happiness, and no one can guarantee that. But everybody ought to have everyone else out of their way as they pursue that. That's the broad philosophy. And then how do you translate that into the complexity of modern life? My first career aspiration was to be a minister, and I believe in the church of the world. This is our church here, and our practice is who we are. The people who go to church on Sunday and pledge

"THIS IS OUR CHURCH HERE, AND OUR PRACTICE IS WHO WE ARE"

their devotion to God and they go out and act like heathens the rest of the week—that just doesn't cut it.

Mark strikes me as someone who works continually to maintain coherence, aligning his beliefs with his actions, his inner life with his outer work. This integrity may be what gave him the ability to continue to govern through all political weather, and to listen for wisdom as much as he spoke.

"My ideas came from the people, not from some higher source. My best ideas came from people all over the state," he says. "I wasn't the most charismatic or articulate spokesman for my causes, but if I had the right cause, it sort of sold itself. That's another saying: Nothing convinces like conviction. If you do believe it truly, that comes across."

The past few years have brought changes to Mark's life, and even to his sense of purpose; but he continues the practices that have afforded him clarity all along.

I don't have any power now. I'm as powerless as any other citizen. And that was a big shift, to go from being governor and having all that authority and all that support staff and all that everything to living in an apartment by myself. My purpose in life had been through my public office, holding it, striving for it, and suddenly it was all over. I knew mentally that it was going to end. But there's no way you can be emotionally prepared for that shift. You just have to go through it.

When I was governor, I remember just sitting in bed at night, just closing my eyes and praying for the wisdom to know what's the right thing to do and the courage to do it. But you need some kind of foundation of spirituality and belief, this power that's greater than us and some way to tap into that and some way to reconcile the horror of your life with a belief in something greater and better than we are. And that's a struggle. I haven't mastered that by any means. And I don't view myself as a paragon of wisdom or virtue.

> "**BUT YOU NEED SOME KIND OF FOUNDATION OF SPIRITUALITY AND BELIEF, THIS POWER THAT'S GREATER THAN US AND SOME WAY TO TAP INTO**"

Mark Dayton is a perfect example of someone who, early on, aligned with his purpose. By trusting himself and his calling and guidance, he accessed genius and he created incredible achievements in this world. So many aspects of his journey were not easy, but Mark Dayton had a why, a powerful purpose, and millions of people are better because of it.

The path to purpose

I recently met a potential client who is sharp, smart, and ambitious. He wanted help getting to the next level, becoming the next Steve Jobs. It's not uncommon at all for my practice to attract ambitious geniuses and I love the challenge and confidence they present. When people say things like that, I don't laugh at them; I always say, "If you're crazy enough to dream about it, you're crazy enough to make it happen." However, this was different. I always ask a series of questions to get at why they want what they want. Very soon, I realized the true motivation of this particular client. He wanted to build a $1 trillion company and be the most well-known entrepreneur in the world. Great! However, what was driving this desire, and what was the effect of this drive on his life? For this individual, the real motivation was to become famous; he was going to forgo family, love, sleep, and friendship because he said these things were, "a waste of time." It turned out that he has had many disappointments in life and is still influenced by the echo of a father to whom he wanted to prove that he was "worthy". A desire to be seen and acknowledged as successful motivated him; he believed that was going to be the source of his happiness. He is a brilliant man who will undoubtedly do great things in the world, but when the main driver in life is the hunger for fame, which ego drives, it can be destructive—not just to the individual but also to humanity at large. Where does this deep obsession with fame come from, and why do we believe it is a key to happiness? Deep down, it almost always comes from a sense of unworthiness and a profound need to be loved and to be seen. What we fail to realize is this: those feelings will never go away no matter how famous we become.

"**AMERICANS SPEND MONEY THEY DON'T HAVE TO BUY THINGS THEY DON'T NEED TO IMPRESS PEOPLE THEY DON'T LIKE**"

As humans, we desperately need meaning. Mainstream recipes for happiness call for external ingredients—money, fame, possessions. True happiness can always be found right here, right now. Deepak Chopra once posted on Twitter[67] that Americans spend money they don't have to buy things they don't need to impress people they don't like.

---

67. Chopra, D. (2012, June 12). Twitter post. https://twitter.com/deepakchopra/status/212712788903202816

We are social beings who need to get along with one another to survive and prosper. However, there's a danger. We tend to conflate others' lives and purposes with our own. When we do that, we begin to measure ourselves according to others' approval. For example, sometimes I notice I'm not making as much money as some of my big-shot corporate friends are. I think of the nicer home I could have, and the fancier car—the list goes on. But I already have an amazing home, and I love my car. I have an incredible life filled with harmony and a deep sense of purpose. As I write this, I'm sitting in my backyard, incredible greenery and flowers surrounding me. The birds are singing. It's a beautiful day. Bunnies are hopping in and out of the yard, the squirrels are chasing each other, and they're all playing together. I look at my statue of St. Francis of Assisi and I am filled with wonder and gratitude for this particular moment. What more do I need? When we have meaning and purpose in our lives, striving for external outcomes dissipates.

Start by acknowledging what is currently present in your life (even if unpleasant) and then, start asking questions. Start reading and talking to people. Start daydreaming about the things that bring you joy. Start writing. Think about those times when you were content. Look at who you are authentically and what your values are.

Our lives will always feel hollow if we lack the sense that our existence has meaning. This can be an arduous journey at times, full of questioning and discomfort. Sometimes we find ourselves walking the path to our own sense of purpose for years. The effort is worth it, though; we become vessels for something great, and we come to understand the symphony of life. We know why we do what we do, and we have a sense of inner peace very few come to know.

All challenges and difficulties are an invitation to wake up, realize our purpose and our potential, and find

ALL CHALLENGES AND DIFFICULTIES ARE AN INVITATION TO WAKE UP, REALIZE OUR PURPOSE AND OUR POTENTIAL, AND FIND ALIGNMENT

alignment. There is a great awakening happening. People all over the world are realizing that they don't have to live a life in a straitjacket, and they can actually pursue the lives of which they've dreamed. Many of us are reevaluating what matters to us. Business as usual isn't cutting it—and that can be a grand thing. We must continue to ask questions: What if? Why am I here? What makes me happy? The most important question of all is: How may I be of service to others? How can I contribute to this world? Our level of fulfillment is so much greater when our existence and our actions benefit others. Patterns of self-indulgence and self-prioritization have eroded our self-esteem. It's meaningful to be of service to others and make an impact, more meaningful than slaving to get that fancy car. Our effect on others creates a lasting legacy that the accumulation of material possessions never will.

Take the leap anyway

Every time we move out of our comfort zone, it's a stretch. But it's in these moments that we grow more resilient and confident, and we become an active participant in our lives. Even when you feel self-conscious or afraid, take the leap anyway. What have you been wanting to try and just never had (or made) the time for? What are you drawn to repeatedly? What would you do or pursue if you believed you could be successful and happy with it?

Jeanette Dorazio, CEO of software company Leadpages, spoke to me about the power and importance of taking that leap—and of supporting people around us to take leaps and make their own changes.

"I spend a lot of time coaching and encouraging," she says and continues:

I think that's the big thing, encouragement, because people are afraid to take that leap. Often, I will tell people, what's the worst that can happen? Give me the worst-case scenario. They'll tell me, and I say, okay, well now you know what that is. So, if that happens, you'll be prepared. But maybe it won't happen. Maybe something great will come out of it.

Your life is a blank canvas. You can paint it whatever way you want, but the first step is to decide what kind of paintbrush you want to use. It's time for you to start thinking about what kind of life you want. What do you really want out of this? When you know that, the rest becomes effortless in some ways, as clarity and purpose propel you into action.

Here's your chance. So many clients come to me saying they have no idea what their purpose is. Then, after asking them a few questions and talking to me for 15 minutes, it becomes so clear to me what they really want. They know it too but are afraid to see it because it may be too grand, may seem dumb or impossible to them, or they simply aren't free to voice it because then they would have to do something about it.

There has never been a better time to change course and to experiment with new things. This is not the time to hold onto what worked before. This is not the time to give into fear. This is the universe giving you permission to try and to fail, experiment, search, and try again.

By now, if you have read my previous chapters, you know the world is not falling apart and that you have been able to focus on the things that are good and working out for you. Your energy is probably higher. When you have escaped the circle of fear and everyday anxiety, it is time to fulfill your potential and show yourself what you are made of. I do believe we have all been made for a certain type of work; we all play a role that serves humanity. As we do that, the side effect is that we become fulfilled and happy. Waiting to

WAITING TO RETIRE TO DO WHAT YOU WANT TO DO IS A DEATH SENTENCE

retire to do what you want to do is a death sentence. You could be doing it all along the way. Please don't tell me that a sense of purpose is a privilege. My life is a living example of the power of hard work and the investment of years to find "it." I gave up on many lucrative things coming my way because they did not align with my purpose. Although I may have missed out on things that society would deem successful, I have found meaning, purpose, freedom, inner peace, and an escape from the rat race, the stress of which caused me to have nine miscarriages and many health issues. I confronted something so painful I had to act—and I changed my life as a result.

Exercise: Purpose

To live a life of purpose, you have to become crystal clear about who you are and what matters most and to see yourself and your life in a new way. On my website, you can access The Purpose Compass Formula[68]—it's fabulous (and free!) online course that shows you step by step how to live a life of purpose: know yourself, understand what you want and pursue the life you desire. It's about letting go of things we think will bring us joy and find authentic sources of meaning and fulfillment (even if that means our friends might not agree with it!).

---

68. www.jasnaburza.com/formula

" *We are just vessels. And that experience gives us the sense of inner fulfillment. We're not insecure, feeling that we have to have credit. We have that interconnectedness, that inner contentment. But through us can flow the wisdom of the ages. We have everything that we really ultimately want as human beings. It's a full expression of who we are or what we came here to do.*

CHAPTER 12

Tapping the Genius Within: Mediocrity is Self-Inflicted and Genius is Self-Bestowed[69]

The imagination of a person is but the window or door which, when thrown open, lets the divine life stream into our lives. When it is thus thrown open a person is brought into a condition of consciousness which, for want of a better word, is called inspiration. This heavenly inspiration is what links a person to the divine and brings into existence our poets, composers, prophets, mystics, seers, and saints.

—Glenn Clark

To advance humanity, we need genius. That genius is inherent in every single being, albeit often masked and forgotten. We are trained to participate in this world according to set rules that keep most people in

---

69. Quote by Walter Russell

shackles. Finish school, get a job, make money, get stuff—this path of which we are told to follow will lead to material and personal success, but is narrow and it does not allow us time to rest, reset, or create. We have become enslaved without knowing that is the case.

Years and even centuries later, we are still admiring and referencing the genius of people such as Michelangelo, da Vinci, Tesla, and Einstein, just to name a few; but the highly socialized mind limits our genius. We have forgotten—if we ever learned—the art of *curiosita*, the value of which Leonardo da Vinci espoused and tapped into in order to imagine and create his prodigious work.

My coffee table is covered with books of da Vinci's early sketches, ideas, and thoughts, some of which never came to completion and many, like the dream of human flight, that were well before their time. Michael Gelb, the author of *How to Think Like Leonardo da Vinci*,[70] spent decades researching da Vinci's life and work, eventually discerning several principles that guided da Vinci's creative process, principles we can all replicate in these hard times.

When I reread Michael's book, published 24 years ago, I was struck by how relevant and timely it remains. When I mentioned that to Michael, he pointed out that most fundamental truths never go out of style.

By its nature, truth would be true across different cultures, from different traditions, in different languages, different religions. It doesn't matter. When we go back to the ancient Greeks, Socrates, Plato, the birth of philosophy, the love of wisdom is predicated on the focus on three interrelated things: truth, beauty, and goodness. So, philosophy, the love of wisdom, asks a question: How do we find truth? How do we find beauty? How do we find goodness? They're interrelated; they're connected. Throughout human history, the greatest geniuses, the most extraordinary beings who have

---

70. Gelb, M. (2000). *How to Think Like Leonardo Da Vinci*. Penguin.

informed or enlightened or inspired humanity are those who somehow embody, manifest, or express truth, beauty, and goodness. Of those people, Leonardo da Vinci is certainly one of the most extraordinary, and the most well-known.

Michael is one of those people who makes your heart smile: integrous, kind, loving and brimming with *joie de vivre*. From the moment I met him, I knew that he was someone who I wanted to learn from and know. Reading his book is sort of like having Leonardo and Michael mentor you in developing your creative process along the way. I have done the exercises in his book with my children and I am always astounded by how powerful they are.

I would love to be able to paint like Leonardo Da Vinci. I would like to write like Marya Hornbacher. I would like to sing like Beyoncé. These things will likely never happen, no matter how much I might try. The new age gurus saying, "You can do anything" or "Nothing is stopping you from doing what you have always wanted to do," don't consider real-life limitations that exist. Michael says,

> **"IT'S ONE THING TO BELIEVE IN UNLIMITED HUMAN POTENTIAL, IT'S ANOTHER THING TO REALIZE WHAT YOUR LIMITATIONS ARE"**

It's one thing to believe in unlimited human potential, it's another thing to realize what your limitations are. But I realized early on in my life I was not going to make it to the NBA. You could say don't tell me anything's possible, you can do anything. No, I could not play in the NBA even if I trained every day, non-stop, with the best coaches around the clock.

But by attempting to improve on those things, I learned about the process of practice and how to practice well and how to play on a team and how to bring out the best in other people and that served me well. And something that it turns out I did have a very high level of talent for was facilitating a group. So, I wound up becoming one of the best people in the world at doing this. I'm a freaking genius at doing that.

In contrast, there are those people who have incredible talent and many capabilities that remain dormant because they don't know how to cultivate and develop them—or they simply don't believe in themselves.

"IF WE TOOK A LION AND PUT IT IN A CAGE IN THE CIRCUS, COULD WE GET ANY IDEA OF THE ANIMAL'S REAL POTENTIAL?"

In his spiritual primer, Radha Soami Satsang Beas[71] asks: "If we took a lion and put it in a cage in the circus, could we get any idea of the animal's real potential?"

I believe most of us are lions in a cage in a circus of our own making. I have always been fascinated by the question of human potential and what it means for all of us. I know that when not much is asked of me, I'm more likely to take the lazy and easy way out. I also know that when I'm in an environment that sees my potential and allows me to spread my wings, I amaze myself with my capabilities and often wonder where they came from.

The sad truth is that most of us live in an environment of very mediocre expectations, one that does not cultivate genius or call for excellence. Yet, most people I talk to believe deep down that they're

"MEDIOCRITY IS SELF-INFLICTED AND GENIUS IS SELF-BESTOWED."

capable of so much more. They know that they have potential in them to move mountains, to have an impact, and to create lasting change in the world.

Last year, I read the works of Walter Russell and was profoundly moved by his words: "Mediocrity is self-inflicted and genius is self-bestowed."

We sometimes gaze at the sky and *know* we are here for a reason;

---

71. Beas, R. (1997). *A Spiritual Primer*. Lakshmi Offset Printers. https://rssb.org/pdfs/A%20Spiritual%20Primer.pdf

but we often see our brilliance get lost in daily life. We may hide this knowledge so as not to be ridiculed; but in the stillness of a morning, we may wonder what more we could do, and feel perplexed by the disconnect between what we believe ourselves capable of and what we manifest in the material world. That power, that genius, can only be realized when we stop listening to the outside world, tune out its noise, and start nurturing the little voice within.

Learning to access that voice takes time. Michael says,

It's a lifetime of contemplation, exploration and the unknown. This is the real realm of genius, and this is where most people don't develop [that] genius, because they want premature certainty in everything. I'll give you some certainty. Two plus two really does equal four in our universe, with all other things being equal; two plus two does equal four. There are a lot of questions that are like that, that have just one right answer. But those aren't life's most important questions. Life's most important questions are things like, How can I have more truth, beauty, goodness? How can I have more meaning and purpose? What's my soul's destiny? How do I discover it? How do I live it today while also earning a living and meeting all my responsibilities? Those questions mean you're going to have to embrace the unknown.

Modern-day Omar Khayum

When the sultan invaded Iran in 1079, Omar Khayum was 24 years old. The sultan asked Khayum to reform the solar calendar along with a team of scientists. Khayum introduced one of the most precise calendars of all time, the Jalali solar calendar, which was used in Iran until the 19th century. This mathematician, astronomer, philosopher, poet, and genius innovated, solved problems, created, and, in the same breath, talked about love and meaning of life.

Bahram Akradi,[72] chairman and CEO of the Life Time® empire, is in some ways a modern-day Omar Khayum, and someone who continues to defy the odds: a success in the eyes of the world, but also a genius in understanding the power of love and prayer. He believes that our genius lies in finding innovative solutions to our problems without giving in to cynicism or ignorance.

I recently sat down with Bahram for a conversation that ranged from business and quantum physics to genius, the wisdom of mystics, and love. Along the winding way, Bahram gave me a glimpse of the way he sees the world, of his own genius, and of the people by whom he himself is inspired.

> **"SOME PEOPLE FLOW THROUGH LIFE, CONSUMED WITH THE IDEA OF HAVING MORE, COLLECTING EVERYTHING, STRUGGLING TO HOLD ON; THEY BECOME STINGY AND SMALL"**

Some people flow through life, consumed with the idea of having more, collecting everything, struggling to hold on; they become stingy and small. Instead of giving back, they try to dam the flow to have a greater share. Whether the dam bursts or not, there's disharmony that interrupts the natural, ancient rhythm of giving and receiving. It's often hard to recognize the cause of this imbalance in our lives. If life gives us a lot, whether its genes that create a work ethic, parents who sacrificed, an inherited intelligence, we will find ourselves in a place where we can use these gifts to give to others. Some people are like the mighty Mississippi, happily living life large, wanting to change the world in a big, impactful way. Others are happy as smaller tributaries, content to help fewer people, but in a role equally as important.[73]

---

72. Life Time.(n.d.).*Leadership*.https://news.lifetime.life/leadership?item=29928
73. Akradi, B. (n.d.). Lessons from the river. https://bahramakradi.com/river

Bahram is clearly one of those who lives large and changes the world in big, impactful ways. While he is by all accounts a successful businessman, he is equally driven by a deep desire to get people out of their ruts—and right now, almost around the globe, we are. "All eight billion people today are running in opposite direction from each other, and we're canceling each other's power, which is a real mistake" he says. "The world needs to come in alignment and the answer is super simple. It's not complicated. Love is, in my mind, the most divine thing I can think of. You just love something or someone or a creature." Bahram says, "It's like, Why? How so? I think that is divine. We haven't found the chip for love. I think it's divine."

We often hear from very successful people and how they are thankful for the hard times because it makes them stronger and more resilient. It's almost as if it activates the genius we didn't even know was there. Bahram is one of these people who believe this. For years, he worked 90-hour weeks, and at times, it seemed the company might go down the drain, taking him with it. "The very day my son Akiliez was born was the day in 2008 the financial crisis hit. In the months that followed, I was lucky to get three hours of sleep each night, up all the time, searching for solutions to problems unlike any we'd ever faced."

Bahram believed he was doing the right thing because it wasn't about him, it was about the vision with which he started his company despite those close to him telling him to walk away, especially after the pandemic closures in 2020 when his revenue stopped overnight. However, precisely because of the hardships he'd already experienced, he knew that the company was going to be okay with him at the helm. He told me he was ready.

I had one super close friend of mine, 19 years older, who has made hundreds and hundreds of millions of dollars, bought and sold hundreds of companies. He was with me every other day saying, this isn't going to work. Leave now, start all over.

And you can make what you've lost a lot faster if you aren't carrying. Because my net worth got washed out and my ownership of Life Time went from 15 percent to 4 percent. And exactly that statement that he made was the reason I was absolutely certain I was going to do the opposite because it wasn't about me. It was not about me at all. It was about the company.

"**PRESSURE CAN BE YOUR FRIEND IF YOU KNOW HOW TO HANDLE IT**"

And I knew if I would have bailed, the company would have melted. And it was the easiest decision. It wasn't complicated. Pressure can be your friend if you know how to handle it.

That type of mental fortitude is awe-inspiring, and awe is mostly what I felt talking to Bahram. Here I was sitting with one of the most successful people in America who talked to me about grit and hard work but also about love, forgiveness, and physics. He is as rich in his soul as he may be in the bank because of the inner work he has done and continues to do.

One part of his work is clearly the practice of humility. Bahram reminds me that one of the basic tenets of all religions is the importance of learning to forgive. "When I make mistakes, I forgive myself, and I forgive other people very quickly," he says. "I don't forget. But I forgive. And the forgiveness cleanses your heart and lets you go. It transfers your energy into what should be done rather than harboring a bad act."

"**THE PATH TO SUCCESS, MOST OF THE TIME, IS RAPID CORRECTIONS**"

He believes this practice is especially true in leadership, where daily self-correction and letting go are critical. "The path to success, most of the time, is rapid corrections. That's how you find true north. Just understand that you can't always be right. You're not going to be all right. Let it go. Let it go. Correct and go."

His perspective on the widespread decline in mental health is powerful and it is something I have often heard from people who immigrated to this country and are always grateful for how much we do have. He says,

> Our mental health is a function overwhelmingly of being spoiled physically. We take things for granted. I can walk. I can eat when I want to eat. There's food available. I don't have to worry about shelter. I have clean water. I have all these things. When we take our focus away from that goodness, we manufacture issues. Go back to all that is good, take inventory of it, get your gratitude for all that is there, and then focus on what you can do to make things better.

It's not about me. It's not about us. It's bigger than that. This message was repeated throughout our conversation like a haunting refrain. While Bahram is very successful, his emphasis always returns to making a difference in the world. "We experience a higher level of fulfillment in life by moving from helping ourselves to helping the people, community and world around us," he says. To me, this is genius. It's aligning with our purpose, being open to being guided by love and being of service to others on a grand scale.

"WE EXPERIENCE A HIGHER LEVEL OF FULFILLMENT IN LIFE BY MOVING FROM HELPING OURSELVES TO HELPING THE PEOPLE, COMMUNITY AND WORLD AROUND US"

When asked about his own sense of purpose and future goals, he says, "I focus my energy on where I can find a clear path, the path to being able to make a difference. A lot of times I think about the timing; if I am meant to do something bigger in this world, the time will come. I will know when the time is there."

Regarding his advice for those of us who seek clarity on our purpose and path? He recommends, simply find five minutes at the end of every day to think about where you are, where you're going and the impact you're having on the world around you. The missing component, the vital bridge between dream and action, is the higher reason for doing what you do. That higher reason is your vision. That's true for any current project and for your life overall. Only by being conscious of your master plan will you be able to align your day-to-day efforts with your heart's greatest truths. And that will lead you to true satisfaction and success.

And then he left me with the words that I will never forget—a reminder that it all almost always comes back to love. He says,

"WE CAN ACHIEVE GREAT THINGS, BUT TRUE JOY LIES IN THE TIMES WE HAVE WITH OTHERS" The only thing that matters is love. We can seek success, we can achieve great things, but true joy lies in the times we have with others, showing up as a giving, caring person. No matter how much money you have or how many things you have collected, the second you die, you no longer have them. Your ownership of things vanishes as soon as you do. But the love you create in this life lives on long after you are gone.

We are just vessels

Bob Roth says to me,

When a person is unbounded and accessing that quantum field level, the unified field of consciousness, then they know the truth, and that infinite creativity flows through them. Solutions flow through them. It's a beautiful thing. We don't get to take credit. We're honored that nature, which expresses itself in the infinite diversity of the universe, uses us as the source of its expression. We are just vessels. And that experience gives us the sense of inner fulfillment. We're not insecure, feeling that we have to have credit. We have that interconnectedness, that inner contentment. But through us can flow the wisdom of the ages. We have everything that we really ultimately want as human beings. It's a full expression of who we are or what we came here to do.

"THROUGH US CAN FLOW THE WISDOM OF THE AGES"

Genius is no more and no less than our creative force waiting to be expressed. The insights and ideas will come to us and will instruct our steps when we still the noise of the world, expand our coherence and commit to be the force for good. Then, we hear the voice of our soul. We get to hear the ideas, poems, books, innovations, and insights that would have been impossible otherwise. We become conduits of something majestic.

Every time I talk to Michael Gelb, I am reminded of the power of what we consume; this is one of the keys to igniting our own genius. "The people and the influences that you spend the most time with will determine the quality of your life," he says. He continues,

So, if you spend most of your time with people who are unhappy, addicted, way out of shape, angry, complaining, and blaming other people, you're more likely to be that. And if you spend your time

"CHOOSE WHERE YOU INVEST YOUR TIME AND YOUR ENERGY BECAUSE IT DETERMINES THE QUALITY OF YOUR LIFE"

with Jasna and Leonardo da Vinci and Michael, then things will work out much better for you. So, choose where you invest your time and your energy because it determines the quality of your life.

217

After months of reading books on personal development, spirituality, self-help, and science, they all seem to point to one secret: The kingdom of God is indeed within. Genius is inherent; everything I ever want is inside of me, if I only take the time to look.

When a woman is pregnant, there is an incubation period to prepare the mother and the family for the child's arrival. This period is filled with excitement and anticipation, but it's also filled with discomfort and challenges, stretching the woman literally to her max on many occasions. More often than not, it's also filled with pain. It makes sense, doesn't it? To have this period to prepare for the arrival of something so majestic it will completely transform us. We have to be ready. So, if you're sitting here in anticipation of your achievements, genius, and wildest dreams coming true, you have to give yourself an incubation period to prepare for its arrival. If we don't, we will not know how to handle the greatness that befalls us, and we will squander any goodness that comes our way. Because one of the greatest lessons we have failed to realize is this: It's who we become in the process that gives us the joy, not necessarily the outcome. It's you, giving birth to yourself. Like a mother's pain, the pain of becoming ourselves means something; like her, we can be willing to endure it because we know why.

ONCE YOU ACHIEVE YOUR DREAMS, YOU WILL REALIZE THAT THIS ENTIRE TIME YOU HAVE BEEN AFTER THE PERSON WHO REALIZED THE DREAM, NOT THE DREAM ITSELF

Once you achieve your dreams, you will realize that this entire time you have been after the person who realized the dream, not the dream itself. There is an incredible freedom that befalls you once you exit the mainstream expectations of "efforting" and getting there in non-authentic ways.

Board of directors

Have you ever wondered why you like very specific things? Who do you look up to, alive or dead? Who inspires you the most? What ideas, concepts, or things appeal to you that you can't explain? Let me give you an example of eccentric and fascinating things and the people who do it for me. I am fascinated by flamenco, music, fashion, priesthood, incredible art, Leonardo da Vinci, holy texts—all of them, interior design, beautifully manicured gardens, forest bathing, people who took uncharted paths, Eastern philosophies, high heels, forests, praying, makeup, beautiful textiles, Jesus and Mohammed and Buddha, Italy, traveling the world, Oprah Winfrey, Napoleon Hill and Walter Russell, beautiful jewelry, quantum physics, healing techniques, technology, pickleball, dancing the night away... I hope you can see how unique this list is. I bet you have your own list. We all do. It's within this list that you will find secrets about yourself. The things that pull you without expectation or explanation. The things that bring you joy and solace, those are the things that have secrets to tell you.

One of the things that has been incredibly helpful to me is to evoke the energy of the people who share similar interests and bring them into my household. How? By creating my own board of directors: a list of people who inspire me, fascinate me, and exhibit some of the idiosyncrasies apparent in my list. This was an idea Napoleon Hill suggested after he spent decades interviewing the world's most successful people. He called them "invisible counselors." My own invisible counselors include Napoleon Hill, Steve Jobs, Jesus, Buddha, Mohammed, Einstein, Oprah, Rumi, Walter Russell, Wayne Dyer, Saint Francis of Assisi, Frida Kahlo, Leonardo da Vinci, Nikola Tesla, Mother Teresa, Sophia Loren, and more.

The insights of Glenn Clark seem relevant here. In *The Soul's Sincere Desire*,[74] he writes,

---

74. Clark, G. (1926). *The Soul's Sincere Desire*. Little Brown, and Co.

The imagination of a person is but the window or door which, when thrown open, lets the divine life stream into our lives. When it is thus thrown open a person is brought into a condition of consciousness which, for want of a better word, is called inspiration. This heavenly inspiration is what links a person to the divine and brings into existence our poets, composers, prophets, mystics, seers, and saints.

IMAGINATION, HEAVENLY INSPIRATION—AND QUANTUM PHYSICS? YES.

Imagination, heavenly inspiration—and quantum physics? Yes. If we go ahead and play with the notion that there really is no time, no before or after in a sequential manner, then I should be able to access the energies and the intelligence of those who came before me. I believe the sage advice and intelligence of the people who inspire me is always accessible to me; I only have to ask. I have created a collage of images of these individuals and hung it in my office in a nicely created frame; this is my board of directors. These are the people I expect to guide me and give me inspiration and answers to the question I'm seeking. I talk to them when I need to come up with an idea or if I'm struggling with a decision. I ask for their guidance as I write these words in hope that some of their magic will be translated into this book in a modern way so we can understand and have access to it.

Think about creating your own board of directors. Who are the people who you look up to? What concepts or philosophies attract you? I bet the list is going to be radically different from mine, and if you're honest, it's going to reflect the most truthful and authentic parts of yourself. Creating this list will make you feel at home. This is not for others; you don't have to post it on social media. It's your private collection of mentors who can inspire you and give you guidance every step of the way. You are invoking the power of intention and aligning yourself with the values and principles these individuals held; we are a product whatever we hold in mind. Go ahead and make your list. Find their images online and create a collage that you frame, or even just keep on your phone. Let it be a resource to guide you on your path. When struggling with a decision, imagine what they would do and how they would do it. Napoleon Hill believed these sessions with our board of directors made us more "receptive to ideas, thoughts and knowledge" that could come to us through intuition. You will find that almost every one of the individuals to whom you are drawn expressed the belief that all of us are capable of greatness. They understood the secret; they took the time to nurture the genius within, and they are now allowing you to do the same.

We spend decades delegating our power to others, disregarding any potential within. This came up in my conversation with entrepreneur Hayley Matthews-Jones when she noticed that she shared the same desire and potential with all the people who inspired her. "All those people at that table," she says, "why couldn't I be one of those?" She continues,

> They're no smarter than me. They may have had better, easier opportunities, but when you sit down at those important tables of those world leaders, you realize they put their pants on one leg at a time like everyone else, and they don't have anything more to contribute because of their job title. Like, they just had a different life experience, right? And so, try to channel some of that. Like, why not me? What if I walk through this door and it's the best room I've ever been in?

"What if I walk through this door and it's the best room I've ever been in?"

The stroke of genius comes in stillness

In my search for healing, I came across a man who claimed dowsing is a tool for spiritual advancement. Joey Korn started as a dowser some 30 years ago in Georgia, and he has since completely turned the dowsing world upside down through his work with energies and the assumption that humans create discordant energies. Last year, I went to a retreat Joey Korn and his wife held because I wanted to learn more. Joey says that most of the insights in his work, the big discoveries in his career, and his ideas for books have come to him through moments of awe.

These moments can be replicated, and here's how: Joey talks about something he calls "relaxitation." It is a process of relaxing the body, mind, and soul. It's a form of meditation but with one caveat: you pose a question or ask for guidance before you start your "relaxitation." Every day after we had lunch, he would ask us all to ponder difficult decisions in our lives or a question that we have been struggling with and to ask that we be given the guidance or answers that we need. Notice what Joey was doing there was setting an intention before the practice of "relaxitation." By now, you know that intention is molding the physical manifestation or physical world, and that world deeply cooperates with our subconscious. After we would set an intention, we would get into a very comfortable position, some sitting down and some laying down, and for 22 minutes we would surrender our questions to our intention, fully trusting that the answers would come. He was teaching us how to cultivate theta waves, a brain state in which we are easily influenced and inspired when the conscious mind takes a break.

Another author whose work made a profound impact on my life is Walter Russell. Russell was an accomplished sculptor, painter, entrepreneur, architect, and philosopher who believed that everyone has consummate genius within them. In *The Message of the Divine Iliad*,[75] Russell writes,

We all inherit ALL that God has to give. The maximum of genius is in everyone. A spoonful is not given to one and a

---

75. Russell, W. (1971). *The Message of the Divine Iliad* (vol. 1 and 2). University of Science & Philosophy.

bowlful to another and a bushel to another. We are all born equal in the Light of God. We are his omniscient Light, and all of it centers in us. The only difference between the greatest genius in the world

> "THE MAXIMUM OF GE-NIUS IS IN EVERYONE. A SPOONFUL IS NOT GIVEN TO ONE AND A BOWL-FUL TO ANOTHER AND A BUSHEL TO ANOTHER."

and the ordinary man is that the genius is aware of the Light within him and the ordinary man is not aware of that Light. The omnipotent Light is in everyone—all of it—in all of its fullness. Likewise, all knowledge is in the Light of everyone, awaiting one's awareness of it. All who desire to thus awaken their inherent genius may do so by thus desiring to awaken it.

(A side note: I have come a long way in my understanding of God since my early days as a devout Moslem reading the Qur'an. To me, God is whatever highest force of unconditional love exists in your life—one that doesn't punish or make you burn for eternity. I can find that invisible force all around me, in humans and in nature.)

The genius within is simply our creative force wanting to be expressed. The insights and ideas will come to us and will instruct our steps when we still the noise of the world, expand our coherence, and commit to be the force for good.

If you want to tap into genius and greatness and to create in a way that will have amazing impact, it will come from your highest source, not from the programs installed by experience or from the society in which you live. Those programs—the beliefs, stories, memories you carry—act like a bad bug on a computer, slowing down everything and clogging our ability to produce good work or works. The goal is to clear these programs and influences forever and tap into the source from which all inspiration and manifestation comes. This is important: you can do this yourself. Every single one of us can do this.

Success and purpose come naturally when we remove the programming. Otherwise, we only repeat the cycle, moving in the same patterns repeatedly, and wondering why we can't seem to break through. We decide that we aren't good enough, smart enough—none of that is true. The truth is that we are dragged down by a bug in our operating system. The first step is awareness, then the willingness to do something about it. Once you intend to clear it, you just have to follow the steps you will undoubtedly receive from inspiration.

Intending

In the early mornings when the world is still asleep, I know the truth. The truth of oneness, gentleness, and love. The truth that cannot be sold or bought but can only be realized through inner work. You and

YOU AND I ARE ONE, CONNECTED BY A TAPESTRY THAT PERMEATES EVERY NOOK AND CRANNY

I are one, connected by a tapestry that permeates every nook and cranny. Quantum physicists call it the Higgs field, but it's also called Universe, God, Allah, Akasha— that which can be found everywhere. We all have access to it and can use it to create a peaceful, purposeful, and love-filled life. This happens in an instant. Yet, we must show up daily to surrender all false narratives, judgments, and desires sold to us by the marketing machine that makes our self-esteem dependent on the latest trend.

As we enter today, walk with me. Let's say: "I do not need to be anxious about anything. I trust I will be guided and will know what to do and where to go, to whom I should speak and what I should say, what thoughts to think, what words to give to the world. The safety that I bring is given to me."[76]

---

76. Foundation for Inner Peace (1975). *A course in miracles.* Foundation for Inner Peace.

May your day be blessed and intentional because intention guides your day and life. Resist the urge to delegate your power to nicely branded accounts promising joy when they know not what joy is. You don't need a course for it. You just need an open heart, quiet time, and intention to connect with this field that will bless you and everyone around you. That is the true manifestation we all want.

Morning incantation practice

The way you start your day directs the energy of that day. What are some of the things to affirm and pay attention to? What is the overall intention for the next 24 hours? Envision your day before you begin. Grounding yourself before the day starts is one of the most important aspects of keeping your coherence in a world where the incoming barrage of demands never stops. It can be as simple as, "My intention for the day is to just remember to breathe" or "I will move with grace in a day full of demands."

> "MY INTENTION FOR THE DAY IS TO JUST REMEMBER TO BREATHE"

Evening incantation practice

What went well, what do I want more of or less of? How can I evoke the presence of Source tomorrow? How do I do that better? How do I start again? We know that whatever we ingest (our mental diet) for the last hour or so before bed is what we let our subconscious marinate in for the next 6-8 hours. Train your brain to go to bed with something enjoyable and constructive. Ask a question or journal before you go to bed and remember there is a part of you that never sleeps. A part of you is aware, even while you sleep, and that part will follow the intention you set.

> *Whatever way we define healing, it doesn't take place until our deepest selves are engaged. We may heal superficially, on the physical level, but to truly heal is to change and awaken and evoke deeper parts of ourselves, those we sometimes can't even explain. This type of healing leaves ripples in its wake. This type of healing opens the way to purpose, meaning, and genius; it allows us to be of service to others and to help others heal.*

13

We Have Been Healing All Along

Healing requires one thing above all: it takes action. This will not be done for you. Eventually you, yourself, will have to choose how to do it, how to live. You will have to find your way.

—Marya Hornbacher

What if there was nothing to be fixed?

Some time ago, a friend recommended I see a regression therapist who would use hypnosis to access previous lives that might explain certain tendencies or personality traits. I am always interested in exploring new things, so I eagerly awaited my appointment. The woman I met was lovely and, as a friend of a friend, I trusted her. I don't remember all of the details, but she put me in a hypnotic state and guided me to the previous life most relevant to my current life.

In this state, I was aware of myself as a little girl, aged 5 or 6. I was walking down a corridor that looked like a monastery. To the right, there were arches that led to the most beautiful garden full of sunshine, flowers, and wildlife. This was where I was headed when the therapist asked me to look to the left and find the door. Suddenly, a door appeared, and as I walked in, I became very scared. I entered a room filled with dusty bottles that appeared to hold magic potions. The room was dark, and I didn't like being there. I kept saying *I want out, I don't belong here*, but the therapist kept encouraging me to go in deeper. I saw a man with a black hood over his head bent over one of the counters, perhaps working on a potion; it looked like he was up to no good. The therapist kept suggesting that I look at what he was doing and asking what he looked like, but my little body just screamed in protest. I couldn't see and I didn't want to. I said I wanted out, so she led me out into the corridor and asked me to go into another door. I refused because I saw the most beautiful woman walking toward me, and I knew that was my mother. She wore a long white dress and had white lace in her beautifully curled long hair. She gave me a big hug, then took my hand and led me into the garden. To this day, I can close my eyes and see it: lush greenery everywhere, the most beautifully manicured gardens with trellises, all types of flowers, birds, and bunnies. She took both of my hands; we were dancing and moving in circles and it was pure joy. At one point, I remembered the room. I stopped and looked at the door and then at my mother. She knew what I had seen, but she smiled a big smile and said, "If you don't look there, it can't touch you. If you don't go in there, it can't touch you. For as long as you don't open that door, you are safe. That is not for you. Come dance with me in the garden. This is where you belong. Stay in the garden." I instantly felt safe; relieved, I continued dancing with her in that beautiful place.

This experience shook me to the core because of its message. I don't know if past lives are real, and I don't know if that vision was really me with my mother. However, the imagery led me there in my mind, and it told me something that was affirming both for me and for the work I do with my clients: We are constantly looking for something to fix. Our entire economy is focused on having something to fix.

But what if there is nothing to fix? What if constantly looking for the door with scary men concocting potions is how we actually create something to fix? What happens if we don't focus there? What if instead we assume the best is yet to come?

WHAT IF THERE IS NOTHING TO FIX?

When I first got rid of my TV decades ago, then stopped reading the newspapers that were part of my morning routine, and then later took a break from social media, I was met with pushback. People told me I couldn't just be a hermit, that I had to educate myself and be an informed citizen. However, I was happier in my garden. I was happier with a book I chose to read, with the music I listened to while I did housework, with time spent playing with my children. My husband often tells me I live under a rock because I often don't know what is happening in our city, but if it's important to my existence and wellbeing, I imagine someone will inform me. We have to ask ourselves, what is really important to us?

The more I research I do and the older I get, the more certain I am that healing—full alignment with the self—comes from coherence. That coherence and alignment comes from removing the excess that weighs us down so that we can return to coherence and homeostasis.

A healer is one who restores or repairs; healing can be defined as the process of becoming well again. Some other definitions that come to mind: to heal is to make whole, make better, become sound, restore to purity, and to be relieved of distress.

Whatever way we define healing, it doesn't take place until our deepest selves are engaged. We may heal superficially, on the physical level, but to truly heal is to change and awaken and evoke deeper parts of ourselves, those we sometimes can't even

TO TRULY HEAL IS TO CHANGE AND AWAKEN AND EVOKE DEEPER PARTS OF OURSELVES

explain. This type of healing leaves ripples in its wake. This type of healing opens the way to purpose, meaning, and genius; it allows us to be of service to others and to help others heal.

THERE IS NO ONE PATH TO HEALING. THERE IS ONLY *YOUR* WAY. There is no one path to healing. There is only *your* way. Your way of healing arises from who you are, from your needs and your instincts, from your goals and intentions, from what resonates with you.

The impulse to heal comes to us in many forms. Most often, it comes after a profound ask for help. It comes in a moment of great pain or pressure, and it sets us off on a journey to the self. This is why we must give thanks for the moments of suffering; they are gifts in disguise.

Not everyone wants to heal

In her book *Why People Don't Heal and How They Can*,[77] Carolyn Myss writes,

> It has become apparent to me that assuming that everyone wants to heal is both misleading and potentially dangerous. Illness can, for instance, become a powerful way to get attention you might not otherwise receive; as a form of leverage, illness can seem almost attractive. Illness may also convey the message that you have to change your life quite drastically. Because change is among the most frightening aspects of life, you may fear change more intensely than illness and enter into a pattern of postponing the changes you need to make.

We often believe that the best way to support others is to corroborate their sad stories and to add fuel to the drama; we all bond over the chaos in our lives. So many of us lose friends when we are not

---

77. Myss, C. (1998). *Why People Don't Heal and How They Can*. Harmony.

willing to listen to their woeful tales because we are seen as lacking in compassion or understanding. I believe the greatest gift we can give to others is to offer an alternative response to the endless outpouring of complaint and blame. That offers no healing; it only creates a recursive loop of more trauma and chaos.

I worry that we conflate our traumas and scars with our character and ourselves, and that we use trauma as an excuse to throw tantrums with impunity. However, life has so much more to offer when we decide to heal those wounds and overcome the challenges we've faced. We will come to realize the real, true, authentic power we possess.

We found our way down here. Now we will find our way out

Imagine a life of being in an out of hospitals for years, struggling with anorexia, bulimia, alcoholism, suicide attempts, drug addiction, and bipolar disorder. For decades. Until her late 30s, for *New York Times* bestselling author, journalist, and teacher, Marya Hornbacher, that was just life. I inhaled Hornbacher's two memoirs, *Wasted*[78] and *Madness*.[79] They were honest, raw, and brilliantly written; they made me feel something at every level of my being.

I read these books as I'd begun writing this one, and for a moment I thought, "This 'We can heal' message is garbage." What about people who suffer to the extent Marya did with mental health concerns or addiction? There was something that Marya said in her memoir *Wasted* that shook me to my core, and it has become a central theme of this book.

She writes,

Healing requires one thing above all: it takes action. This will not be done for you. Eventually you, yourself, will have

---

78. Hornbacher, M. (1999). *Wasted: A Memoir of Anorexia and Bulimia.* Harper.
79. Hornbacher, M. (2009). *Madness: A Bipolar Life.* Mariner.

"HEALING REQUIRES ONE THING ABOVE ALL: IT TAKES ACTION. THIS WILL NOT BE DONE FOR YOU." to choose how to do it, how to live. You will have to find your way. I don't know that everyone will; of course I don't know that. I do know that no one who does recover does so by accident. Recovery is a choice. I can sit around hoping for recovery till I'm blue in the face. But until I start putting the pieces together—investigating treatment options, exploring methods of recovery that have worked for others, trying out methods that might work for me, and putting the ones that work into action on a daily basis—I'm going to stay stuck. So the task is ultimately our own: we need to cobble together a recovery strategy that will work for us. And that really is a process of trial and error, at least for now. Different methods will work well for different people… [W]e each are charged with the task of finding for ourselves the tools that will help us recover. The desire for a quick or obvious fix is ridiculous. We found our way down here. Now we will find our way out.

That message was my guiding light for this book and I am so grateful I had a chance to meet her and work with her. Marya did the work. Repeatedly. Furthermore, healed. Today, she is one of the most fascinating, healthy, and aligned people I know. She is aligned with her. By trial and error, she found her way.

"Even when we were 'sick' or 'broken' or 'in crisis,' we've been healing all along," Marya says to me. These words echo in my mind when I think of what it means to become whole and to find your way back to yourself. With every thought, breath, failure, and choice, we are already healing. Every effort to get better, and every setback as well, is an important and maybe even necessary part of healing. Terms such as "miraculous healing" or "overnight success" are misrepresentations of the long journey that precedes a transformation.

As such, they give false narratives about how we may return to balance after a setback or emotional turmoil. The assumption is that one thing does it or that it's a sudden stroke of insight, when in fact, it has been happening all along even despite any evidence of such a thing. This is precisely why we have to be patient with ourselves and not give up when a few magic tricks that the gurus talk about don't do it for us.

Marya says that healing looks like, "being able truly to integrate not only all parts of oneself, but all the periods in one's life, however messy." According to her, often this process isn't conscious. You just wake up one day and notice that you began to heal. For Marya, more than making a conscious decision to change something, it was about entertaining the idea of,

> What if I changed? What if I even considered changing? What if I entertained the idea that things could be less painful? Suppose I didn't have to suffer this much? What would it look like to suffer less? What would I do to suffer less? Am I willing to entertain even one of these good ideas when I'm so attached to my bad ideas and self-destructive mechanisms? Even though people may suggest things and try to help us, nothing will happen until we decide to entertain these questions, however difficult they may be.

> **"WHAT IF I ENTERTAINED THE IDEA THAT THINGS COULD BE LESS PAINFUL?"**

What she is describing is the concept "curiosita," one of the principles in Michael Gelb's book about thinking like Leonardo Da Vinci. Curiosita begins with asking the right questions. Here's what Michael tells me when I ask him about this:

> The questions you ask every day determine the quality of your life. How can I make my life more beautiful? How can

"THE QUESTIONS YOU ASK EVERY DAY DETERMINE THE QUALITY OF YOUR LIFE" I make the lives of other people more beautiful? I notice that I'm feeling lots of anger and fear and anxiety. What can I do to be free from that? So, the question is the beginning of everything.

These questions create an opening and through that opening, opportunity sneaks in: We start taking actions toward the possibility of "what if." You start to realize that life could be different. In the world where we expect certainty, the process of coming back to ourselves is anything but—it's uncertain and ambiguous, as Marya says: "I will approach every unknown with an attitude of friendly curiosity. I don't know what I'm doing. I don't know how to do this. As a professor, the wisest thing I can say to a student is I don't know. And that freedom to not know is what keeps the doors open. It is liberating."

We really don't know or can guarantee anything, but we can begin to ask questions and entertain the idea of escaping the cage of our own making.

When we have lost heart or are feeling defeated and without a way out, we become settled in that reality and humans are so really well with befriending uncomfortable states of being because it is a state of survival. However, by taking the first step, we get to the next and the next, and soon, we realize that every step has been a significant progress in the right direction, however non-eventful or grand. Comparing this healing journey to her writing craft, Marya says, "E. M. Fortser said that writing a novel is like driving in the fog at night; you have no idea where you're going. You can only see as far as the headlights, but you can make the whole trip that way. That's a great analogy for healing."

In today's world, it is difficult to plan and to see the future clearly because so much of it is uncertain. Refusing to take the first step ensures that we will not make the journey. As inclined we are to take the shortcuts, this process asks us to do the work. We can take many shortcuts in life. Some are very beneficial and will save time and money, and there are shortcuts that will cost you your life. What am I talking about? That the fast pace of life, public progress, and achievement of others that we witness make us susceptible to needing it all *now*. It's normal and to be expected, but I urge us all to resist.

Needing things now makes us take the shortcuts, but there is something valuable about going through it: You can go under the knife and realize that what was inside was the only thing that ever mattered. You can rush to publish that book or make that money, and in the rush of it all, you can forget about those around you, the most important aspects in life in the end. When inclined to take a shortcut, ask yourself: What am I trying to avoid and what do I gain from walking the talk?

> **WHAT AM I TRYING TO AVOID AND WHAT DO I GAIN FROM WALKING THE TALK?**

Purpose over suffering

My mom once told me that the most selfish thing you can do is to do something for someone else. That way, she would argue, you could immediately feel better because you did something for someone else who needed you. Between shifting attention from your pain and doing something good, you feel amazing. One of the things I learned from Marya in many instances is her deep sense of purpose in this world and how many times it was this sense of purpose that pulled her. In our conversation, she references a poem that I had never read before but that left me in tears with its beauty and meaning. It was the poem "Wild Geese" by Mary Oliver.[80]

---

80. The full poem can be found here: http://www.phys.unm.edu/~tw/fas/yits/archive/oliver_wildgeese.html

We all suffer in one form or another, but the beauty and power of nature reminds us how we are part of something so much more majestic and more meaningful than today's struggle. That is what we find in a sense of purpose and in doing something of service for others. To engulf ourselves in our suffering separates us from the magic of nature. In contrast, our connection with it gives us a sense of comfort and a realization that our concerns are indeed just a small part of this grand procession of life that happens without any effort on our part.

We beat up ourselves so much for not being better, for not being like "them," more advanced, more... everything.

Just use life's circumstances to propel yourself forward—like snakes do. Marya says,

> Snakes have to have something to push themselves against in order to move. They have to have a rock or a wall or some dirt or some roughness. They cannot exist without conflict. They can't move without something to move against. And I felt at that time like I was pushing myself off whatever showed up so I could just turn. And it worked.

Even though she feels she has been guided, the guidance came from life:

> Open a book randomly. Something will be there. Not because I think it's being sent to me, but because at that point, the brain, the heart, and the spirit are so open that we will, like the body will, when we're terribly malnourished, take nourishment from anything. So, I started to trust that I was so hungry for guidance that I would just find it anywhere. And I continue to trust that.

I believe that guidance is all around us and it's precisely because of what Marya says: It's because of our openness and willingness that it works.

Marya continues,

> Purposeful acts became my lifeline and I continue to believe that that is what heals. What we've often called mental illness isn't always science. Often it is purpose; often it is a sense of there's something I wish to do, not something I wish to get or take or be given. I wish to *do* something. What are the steps I would need to take to get there? What's the purpose? That's not magic.

The discomfort and the magic of the mundane

Hooked on dopamine and unable to still the chatter, we are constantly on the hunt for what's bigger, bolder, more entertaining, and more engaging. It's avoidance at its best. I know it all too well when the phone data tell me I opened Instagram 10 times in one hour. Yet, sitting in the discomfort is where the magic lies. Part of Marya's healing journey was precisely this:

> You need to be able to deal with the discomfort in the now. And that is a daily practice. For me, meditation isn't optional. What helps me deal with crisis or pain or boredom or discomfort now is the fact that if I can sit for an hour on my ass and stare at the wall through every thought process that is trying to torment me, I can definitely get through an uncomfortable meeting.

"YOU NEED TO BE ABLE TO DEAL WITH THE DISCOMFORT IN THE NOW. AND THAT IS A DAILY PRACTICE."

However, meditation is not a quick fix; it feels anticlimactic when we are feeling the big feelings. The last thing we want to do is meditate when we are facing the things that don't feel good. There has to be a better, bigger, faster fix, right? Not according to Marya: "It feels like there ought to be a big bang that is helpful in the same degree that we are hurting. But in fact, the mitigation of that big hurt is tiny little interventions like doing the dishes that get us through the big stuff."

Talking to Marya, knowing full well what life dealt her, makes me love and respect her even more. She is strong, resilient, and smart, and she has given to this world so much art, so much genius that is rare in today's society. I am infinitely grateful to her for how much impact she has had on my life and for her help, as my editor, in writing this book. In so many ways, this book would not have been possible without her.

Nothing is important until it's important to you

One of the main reasons I left social media in 2020 was the pressure I felt to offer commentary on everything that was happening. Because of my "influence," this level of response was expected of me, it seemed like. Nothing I said seemed right. Either I stood for something or I stood against it. I couldn't seem to do anything right. So, I left. I grew silent, saying nothing but completely withdrawing to tend to my inner garden. I receive dozens of emails or requests to support something every month and to share or speak about it. Many of these are important societal issues, but the assumption is that we all care equally about something that others care about. Then we are made to feel bad because it is "affecting so many people." However, if I were to pay attention to all the sad issues in the world that others bring to my attention, I would be curled up on the floor mid-morning, unable to move because it's simply too depressing. Is that how I help the world? I certainly don't think so. To become the beacons of light, innovators and changemakers, we have to tend to our inner garden, which involves having boundaries and

TO BECOME THE BEACONS OF LIGHT, INNOVATORS AND CHANGEMAKERS, WE HAVE TO TEND TO OUR INNER GARDEN

being disciplined about our mental diet. Years ago, if a gorilla ate someone in another country, you wouldn't even know about it. Today, you are going to be shown those scenes repeatedly. Do you need to see or know that? If there is a tornado coming my way, I would like to know, but I don't have to know about a multi car crash somewhere in Georgia (considering I live in Minnesota). If I do, do I have to see it repeatedly and follow along to see the updates of such loss? This is not to be insensitive. It is to ask yourself how you benefit from that information. Better yet, how does it harm you? Is it worth it? Does it weaken you and make you less capable of tending to those around you and the world?

Not only can we heal, but we must heal. Heal how? In any way that will make us feel better. No

NOT ONLY CAN WE HEAL, BUT WE MUST HEAL

matter what you are feeling—being overwhelmed, feeling pain or loss—none of these things last forever. At least they don't have to. Past the need to indulge in our pain and past the periods when you don't know a way out, past all of that—there is a hallway of light, a shimmer of hope of people who did it. Whether it's reclaiming your worth, setting boundaries, or healing from something more traumatic, you can heal, become whole, coherent, and one with yourself. The question is if you are willing to do so, like Marya said in *Wasted:* "Healing requires one thing above all: it takes action."

Healing is about cleaning the cobwebs. Healing me. It's always about healing me and only me. It is the most selfish way to help others.

239

Some of my favorite people are those who read a book about a man who walked on water and performed all kinds of miracles and they would die for that belief. Yet, they do not believe in their body's ability to heal itself aided by the energy of the aforementioned man.

What this means for us is that our thoughts, emotions, and beliefs have a direct effect on the physical world around us. In other words, we can change the world by changing ourselves.

The good news is that we don't need to be physicists to tap into this power. All it takes is a willingness to experiment with your own mind-body connection. There are many ways to do this: meditation, prayer, affirmations, visualization exercises—it's up to you.

The important thing is this: Don't think of your mind as something separate from your body—they are one and the same. Your mind consists of energy (a quantum field), which means it has the ability to affect matter (your body), and vice versa—if you change something about yourself (your thoughts or feelings), this will have an effect on your physical being.

Just start. Imperfectly

You are not going to get things right every time. How do you stop a car driving 300 mph? Slowly and over time. We first have to come to that neutral state to eliminate the speed and the noise so we can build with intention. This goes for getting ramped up as well and changing anything in your life: you start and then you pick up pace. It's a process. It's something tedious and it doesn't look perfect, but the first step is always the first step. We start going to the gym and immediately we feel like we should run like a gazelle: disciplined, poised, and ready. I love what Dario Otero, an entrepreneur who empowers youth

"TOO MANY PEOPLE SIT IT IN THE DISCIPLINE BEFORE THEY START GOING, AND THEY JUST NEVER START."

through his position as CEO of Youth Lens 360, said: "Too many people sit it in the discipline before they start going, and they just never start."

That's just it; you have to pick one aspect of the healing journey most painful to you and just start.

> "There is no one way. There is no one path. There is only your path, and it is never too late to remember who you are, to come home to the truest expression of yourself.

You Are the One
You Have Been Waiting For

Listen to yourself and in that quietude you might hear the voice of God.

—Maya Angelous

I washed my body carefully so it would be clean and pure, as was the custom. I picked out a dress of my sister's that felt like silk. I wasn't normally allowed to wear her clothes, but tonight was different. It was green, long, and elegant, a very grown-up dress.

I watched Mama in our tiny bathroom, bright lights on her face, carefully applying her makeup. She would close one eye and draw a careful black line near her eyelashes, pat pink lipstick on with her fingertip, and add the rest as rouge on her cheeks. She didn't look like my mom anymore—she looked like a movie star, glamorous and elegant. I wanted to look just like her.

She was different with her makeup on. She laughed more. She looked satisfied, happy with herself. She didn't do that much; she didn't always take pride in herself. Most days, she would wear tattered, ill-fitting, or mismatched clothes. Sometimes we teased her. "Does it look like I have time for myself?" she would say, shooing us with the broom. "Look at all this work."

THE FINAL TOUCH WAS HER HIJAB

The final touch was her hijab.

It was a holy night in the month of Ramadan, and we were going to the mosque. As we left the house, we fell into the dark. The few streetlights were just bright enough to show the way. It was brisk, and we walked with our shoulders straight, Mama's gown fluttering behind her in the breeze. She looked regal and proud.

I was so excited. Hundreds of shoes in front of the mosque told us we weren't early. From the dark, the door opened into such brightness: overhead lights, candles flickering everywhere. The mosque was chilly, built of white stone, but the light and all the people inside made it feel warm. The floors were lined with soft, lush Turkish tapestries. I looked around and admired the beauty of the women, their silk hijabs, their eyes, their gowns, and their perfect makeup. They looked holy.

We found our spots on our knees and carefully positioned our prayer beads in front of us, preparing for prayer. My heartbeat was slowed by rhythmic prayer movements. Evening prayer is the longest. Stand up; recite the prayers in Arabic, words you don't understand but know are good and pure, and make you feel good and pure. Get down on your knees and then bow to God over and over again. Oh, how I loved this ritual. I loved the lights and all the women next to me, bowing in unison, looking and smelling fresh and creating an energy of love, community, acceptance, and purity. Tonight, many were away from their husbands, whose feet smelled, away from their beer, and away from the kitchen and everyday life that was simply not kind to them.

Because tonight was a holy night, the women with the most beautiful voices had been selected to sing "ilahije i kaside" or nasheed—holy songs sang in the same tone, a cappella, that would make your entire body shiver. I still shiver thinking about it. I would normally set my gaze on one woman. There was always one woman who stood out in the way she devoted herself to the singing, her eyes mostly closed, with such reverence for God. She was beautiful. Her expression was so pure—pure ecstasy.

THERE WAS ALWAYS ONE WOMAN WHO STOOD OUT IN THE WAY SHE DEVOTED HERSELF TO THE SINGING, HER EYES MOSTLY CLOSED, WITH SUCH REVERENCE FOR GOD

Getting lost in the vibration of God, being carried by the frequency. I joined in almost always—not in the singing part, because I was told many times I didn't have the voice of these holy women, but in the vibration that made me feel something I never felt anywhere else. God was great. I would often tear up, moved by such beauty. I wished I could sing like that. I wished they knew how I felt during the prayer. I wished they would omit that I couldn't sing and let me be part of this sacred circle. I wished.

It's been 20 years since I prayed that way or went to the mosque. But I still listen to nasheed, the holy songs, and I always manage to enter the frequency of God, feeling pure and holy. It's how I think God feels. I still tear up, close my eyes, and silently move in a way that lets my body feel God. Only this time, I don't wish to be one of the girls singing. I am the girl.

It took me 40 years to remember who I was. It wasn't too late. It's as if the trials and tribulations of my life were perfectly orchestrated to make me into the person I am. That is, I am exactly where I need to be.

There is no one way. There is no one path. There is only your path, and it is never too late to remember who you are, to come home to the truest expression of yourself.

IT IS NEVER TOO LATE TO REMEMBER WHO YOU ARE

All of the people interviewed for this book went through their own trials and hardships. In the sea of uncertainty and the dark night of the soul, the belief that something else is possible leads us all. That inner voice that tells us we can. We saw a lighthouse across the dark and turbulent seas. We have all come to give thanks for that journey because of the lessons we learned, the purpose we found, and the people we served.

We are the ones we have been waiting for.

I share this story for various reasons. First, the careful preparation for an act of prayer is the process of setting an intention. There aren't many things in our lives that require that level of devotion anymore. However, that preparation, physical and mental, does matter. Even though I no longer belong to an organized religion, there is such beauty in creating a space in my home that is my sacred space. For all of us, that sort of space is one where we can let go, cry, pray, and find that energy of offering, surrender, and faith within. We don't have to belong to a religion to do that; prayer is magical because of what it does to us internally, not because we are asking something of someone outside ourselves. It changes us

PRAYER IS MAGICAL BECAUSE OF WHAT IT DOES TO US INTERNALLY

and puts us in a place of a higher vibration, greater coherence, and alignment with ourselves. Create a space like that and make it yours. A corner, a nook, a chair—it doesn't have to be anything extravagant, just a space that will welcome you, where you can immediately remember who you are.

Second, growing up, I learned that some people were more special because they had certain gifts or looked a certain way. For too many years, I delegated my own power to others because I didn't allow myself an opportunity to be "that girl." I counted myself out before I even considered the option. How often do we do that? The shoulds and assumptions and "it's always been that way" defeat our purpose and limit our self-expression. Because I couldn't sing as those women could, I assumed I didn't have as close of a contact to God as they did. It seems so silly, but it's true.

Anoint yourself worthy. Pursue the things that set your soul on fire. You can live a comfortable and safe life,

> **ANOINT YOURSELF WORTHY. PURSUE THE THINGS THAT SET YOUR SOUL ON FIRE.**

but we all know that we would live more meaningful and fulfilling lives if we spread our wings and gave ourselves permission to fly.

What if?

In the end, none of us know the truth. We have beliefs that give us hope, but in the entire vast cosmos of which we are a part, there are a myriad of things we believe in for which we do not have material proof. Our faith, our belief, rests on the inner knowledge we possess.

Here's what I know: The practices I have outlined in this book make me a better person. They make me more disciplined about my thoughts and intentions, more willing to invest my time and energy in people and things that make me feel good, and more authentically able to radiate kindness and love. Already I have lived a life that has been blessed by others and that allows me to bring blessings to them as well. That, right there, gives me everything I could ever hope to have. So I invite you to embark on this journey of conscious creation, one that will improve your life and in turn, bless everyone you meet.

The two most powerful statements in my life are *I love you* and *I don't know.* There are many instances

> **THE TWO MOST POWERFUL STATEMENTS IN MY LIFE ARE *I LOVE YOU* AND *I DON'T KNOW***

when I was sure I was right and I was proven wrong. There are so many things that I don't know. As Bakram Akradi says, "None of us know certain things and we can't prove them. But if they make us feel better and allow us to lead a better life, why not try it?"

There can be a deep knowing inside of us even without certainty. Research increasingly supports the wisdom that mystics have offered us for millennia: Our mind is powerful beyond measure.

I have come to believe. Although there are still things in my life that I haven't figured out, I believe in the almost magical power of my thoughts to shape reality, and I commit my life to this practice. That's what it is—a practice. This isn't magic—though it's worth

> **THAT'S WHAT IT IS—A PRACTICE. THIS ISN'T MAGIC**

noting that many things we once thought were magic are turning out to be scientific fact. As William Tiller said

"Miracles" don't necessarily defy the laws of nature. They're a bit less grandiose than that—instead, a miracle is a phenomenon that was previously considered unimaginable. Witnesses to that miracle are called upon to reframe their assumptions and resolve contradictions. In short, they must start to think about their world in a new light.[81]

I remember lying on my couch, nine months pregnant with my first child, and watching this little being perform acrobatic exercises inside my belly. My belly would contort into the weirdest shapes, and both my husband and I found this absolutely marvelous and mysterious. I understand biology and I understand the mechanics of conception, but carrying a child and then giving birth was a miraculous experience for me. Not only because I was told I was never going to have children but also because I think almost every woman who gives birth feels this sense of awe. A life growing inside of me that was wholly dependent on me. I was at once creating a universe

---

81. Manek, N. (2019). *Bridging Science and Spirit: The Genius of William A. Tiller's Physics and Promise of Information Medicine*. Conscious Creation LLC.

and bearing witness to it. It was miraculous, mysterious—it was both magical and utterly real.

Einstein once said, "The most beautiful and deepest experience a man can have is the sense of the mysterious. It is the underlying principle of religion as well as all serious endeavor in art and science. He who never had this experience seems to me, if not dead, then at least blind."

In this book, I have endeavored to share the practices that have changed my life in the belief that they will be life-changing for you who try them, as well. As you experiment with them and discover which ones bring you into a state of resonance, you will also discover your pathway to genius. Will it work for some people like magic? Absolutely. I ask of you that you don't close the door on any of these approaches; just try. It's not even about what happens on the journey; it's about who you become.

I won't lie. The world looks scary right now. The market. Inflation. Discord. Conflict. Uncertainty. Grief. We have no knowledge of what lies ahead, no sense of security about the future. It's hard to plan. That said, dear one, breathe. Look again. I stand by the statement I made at the beginning of this book: This time of turmoil is a gift.

We need a visionary to help us find our way. To help us heal. Heal one, heal them all.

This is where you come in. As do I.

WE NEED A VISIONARY TO HELP US FIND OUR WAY. TO HELP US HEAL. HEAL ONE, HEAL THEM ALL.

Let's rebuild together. Let's reclaim reverence for the little things, and let's create true abundance. Let's make this a time to tap genius, collaborate, and create, reaching for new sources of wisdom, genius, and depth.

In the end, we all go to the same place and take nothing with us. In the end, most people will have regrets; many will never have had the opportunity or taken the chance to reach a higher state of consciousness, the one that gives us access to heaven on earth. There are only a few who will heed the call and discover the beauty and peace beyond all imagination—the beauty and peace they contain.

You have to do the work

Something plagued me for years: I would read all of the self-help and personal transformation books, get inspired, and often move to action, but then I would return into the world and get sucked into the vortex of chaos again. I was talking about this concept with a good friend of mine, Kari, and she hit the nail on the head: "It's like going to a container store when I feel like I need to get more organized. Just by being in the store I feel so much better instantly, and then I go home and do nothing more about it. It's this temporary fix that doesn't last."

Self-help books can be like that. We have to remember that these books are really about the stage where we're getting ready to get ready. That's not the process; that's the prep. You still have to do the work.

That may be the most important work you ever do. Not only will you reap the practical rewards of healing, growing, and creating change, but also your entire life will be transformed as a result. I am not inviting you to come on a 30-day transformation journey. I am inviting you to join me on a complete paradigm shift that will allow us to redefine purpose, meaning, and success.

THIS IS ABOUT THE REST OF YOUR LIFE.

This is about the rest of your life.

We can do hard things

As I write this, I am in Spain with my sister. Separated by war, we never got enough time together. She's my best friend, my greatest confidante, and someone I admire greatly. Both my sister and I understand pain, loss, and suffering. We've had more than our share of it. As we've talked these past few days about this book, we've discussed how healing is a choice; it is the life impulse trying to express itself.

My greatest belief is in the magic of this universe, the belief that healing is possible. Just when I think I figured out one thing, another one pops up that forces me to uplevel and do some more work. That said, we can heal. Marya says,

> Healing is certainly possible. I think if we let go of the construct that healing has the same arc for everyone, if we let go of the idea that someone else can tell you what healing looks like or what yours should look like or what your end goal is, then, yes, absolutely. We can heal.

There are a host of practices not mentioned in this book that are deeply healing—seek them out. Experiment for yourself. Maybe you just get yourself outside during sunrise and that's all you do for months. Maybe you make intention statements a staple of your day. Maybe you double down on prayer. Maybe you decide to make your work very small for two weeks. The journey to oneness is personal; it has to be aligned with who you are.

THE JOURNEY TO ONENESS IS PERSONAL; IT HAS TO BE ALIGNED WITH WHO YOU ARE

My hope and prayer are that this book will offer comfort, inspiration, and support to people who feel restless; may it help you find your path toward a new tomorrow. I have an incredible amount of love for every person who reads these words. I hope you feel it, find it within yourself, and most important, radiate it into the world.

You are the one we have been waiting for.

References

Akradi, B. (n.d.). Lessons from the river. https://bahramakradi.com/river

Akradi, B. (n.d.). Working with others. https://bahramakradi.com/working-with-others

Barna Group. (2016, September 29). Most Americans believe in supernatural healing. Barna Group. https://www.barna.com/research/americans-believe-supernatural-healing/

Beas, R. (1997). *A Spiritual Primer*. Lakshmi Offset Printers. https://rssb.org/pdfs/A%20Spiritual%20Primer.pdf

Billings, L. (2022, October 4). Explorers of quantum entanglement win 2022 Nobel Prize in Physics. *Scientific American*. https://www.scientificamerican.com/article/explorers-of-quantum-entanglement-win-2022-nobel-prize-in-physics1/

Blakeslee, S. (2012, April 2). Mind games: Sometimes a white coat isn't just a white coat. *The New York Times*. https://www.nytimes.com/2012/04/03/science/clothes-and-self-perception.html

Brusaferria, L., et al. (2022). The pandemic brain: Neuroinflammation in non-infected individuals during the COVID-19 pandemic. *Brain, Behavior, and Immunity, 102*, 89-97. https://www.sciencedirect.com/science/article/pii/S0889159122000472#

Burza, J. (n.d.). *Healer in Heels*. www.jasnaburza.com/healerinheels

Burza, J. (n.d.). *Uplevel together: Interview with Dr. Nisha Manek.* https://jasnaburza.com/condition-your-home-to-feel-like-westminster-abbey-with-nisha-manek/

Burza, J. (n.d.). *Healer in Heels: Formula.* www.jasnaburza.com/formula

Chopra, D. (2012, June 12). Twitter post. https://twitter.com/deepakchopra/status/212712788903202816

Clarey, C. (2015, September 14). Novak Djokovic's winning strategy: Mind over chatter. *New York Times.* https://www.nytimes.com/2015/09/15/sports/tennis/novak-djokovics-winning-strategy-mind-over-chatter.html

Clark, G. (1926). *The Soul's Sincere Desire.* Little Brown, and Co.

Clear, J. (2018). *Atomic Habits: An Easy and Proven Way to Build Good Habits and Break Bad Ones.* Avery.

Covey, S. (2020). *7 Habits of Highly Effective People: 30th anniversary edition.* Simon & Schuster.

Diamond, J. (1980). *Your Body Doesn't Lie.* Warner Books.

Dossey, L. (1995). *Healing Words: The Power of Prayer and the Practice of Medicine.* HarperOne

Einstein, A. (2005). Letter, February 12, 1950. In A. Calaprice (Ed.). *The New Quotable Einstein.* Princeton University Press.

Ford, E. (n.d.). *itsEmily.* [Podcast]. https://www.itsemily.com/podcast/

Foundation for Inner Peace. (1975). *A course in miracles.* Foundation for Inner Peace.

Frankl, V. (2006). *Man's Search for Meaning.* Beacon Press.

Gelb, M. (2000). *How to Think Like Leonardo Da Vinci.* Penguin.

Gibran, K. (2019). *The Prophet.* Penguin.

Hajo, A., & Galinksy, A. (2012). Enclothed cognition. *Journal of Experimental Social Psychology, 48*(4), pp. 918-925.

Hansen, S. (n.d.). My thought coach. https://www.mythoughtcoach.com/

Harvard Medical School. (2019, July 1). A 20-minute nature break relieves stress. *Harvard Health Publishing.* https://www.health.harvard.edu/mind-and-mood/a-20-minute-nature-break-relieves-stress

Hawkins, D. (2020). *The Map of Consciousness Explained: A Proven Energy Scale to Actualize Your Ultimate Potential.* Hay House Inc.

Hawkins, D. (2014). *Power vs. Force: The Hidden Determinants of Human Behavior.* Hay House Inc.

HeartMath Institute. (n.d.). Science of the heart: Exploring the role of the heart in human performance. https://www.heartmath.org/research/science-of-the-heart/energetic-communication/

HeartMath Institute (n.d.). *HeartMath Institute.* https://www.heartmath.org/

HeartMath. (n.d.). *Raising our vibration to access our higher potentials.* https://www.heartmath.com/add_heart_call/raising-our-vibration-to-access-our-higher-potentials/

HeartMath Institute. (n.d.). *The science of coherence: Why does coherence matter?* https://www.heartmath.org/heart-coherence/science/

Heisenberg, W. (n.d.). *Quotes.* Goodreads. https://www.goodreads.com/quotes/896047-t-he-atoms-or-elementary-particles-them-selves-are-not-real-they

Henry, M. (n.d.). *Face Foundrié.* www.facefoundrie.com/about

Hornbacher, M. (1999). *Wasted: A Memoir of Anorexia and Bulimia.* Harper.

Hornbacher, M. (2009). *Madness: A Bipolar Life.* Mariner.

Hornbacher, M. (2014). *Wasted: A Memoir of Bulimia and Anorexia* (updated edition). Harper Perennial.

Hunt, C. (2021). *Your Spark is Light: The Quantum Mechanics of Human Creation.* Independently published.

Korn, J. (2004). *Dowsing: A Path to Enlightenment.* New Millennium Press.

Lee, M.-S., Lee, J., Park, B.-J., & Miyazaki, Y. (2015). Interaction with indoor plants may reduce psychological and physiological stress by suppressing autonomic nervous system activity in young adults: a randomized crossover study. *Journal of Physiological Anthropology, 34*(21).

Lembke, A. (2021). *Dopamine Nation: Finding Balance in the Age of Indulgence*. Dutton.

Li, Q. et al. (2022). Effects of forest bathing (shinrin-yoku) on serotonin in serum, depressive symptoms and subjective sleep quality in middle-aged males. *Environmental Health and Preventative Medicine, 27*(44). doi: 10.1265/ehpm.22-00136

Life Time. (n.d.). Leadership. https://news.lifetime.life/leadership?item=29928

Macmillan Dictionary. (n.d.). Infobesity. https://www.macmillandictionary.com/buzzword/entries/infobesity.html

Manek, N. (2019). *Bridging Science and Spirit: The Genius of William A. Tiller's Physics and Promise of Information Medicine*. Conscious Creation LLC.

Middendorf, N. (n.d.). Live it list. https://nicolemiddendorf.com/live-it-list/

Myss, C. (1998). *Why People Don't Heal and How They Can*. Harmony.

Prema, G. (2022). *It's All Light: Juicy Science Meets Spirituality Without Religion*. Independently Published.

Radin, D. (2018). *Real Magic: Ancient Wisdom, Modern Science, and a Guide to the Secret Power of the Universe*. Harmony.

Roth, B. (2018). *Strength in Stillness: The Power of Transcendental Meditation*. Simon & Schuster.

Rumi, J. (1999). *Hush, Don't Say Anything to God: Passionate Poems of Rumi*. Jain Publishing Company.

Rumi, J. (2022). *Rumi: Drop of Enlightenment*. Independently published

Russell, W. (1971). *The Message of the Divine Iliad* (vol. 1 and 2). University of Science & Philosophy.

Schiffman, R. (2016, November 16). Are trees sentient beings? Certainly, says German forester. *YaleEnvironment360*. https://e360.yale.edu/features/are_trees_sentient_peter_wohlleben

Selhub, E., & Logan, A. (2014). *Your Brain on Nature*. Collins.

Stapp, H. (2011). *Mindful Universe: Quantum Mechanics and the Participating Observer* (2nd ed.). Springer.

Sunlight Institute. (2023). The sun & UV light. https://sunlightinstitute.org/the-sun-and-uv-light/

Thoreau, H. D. (2009). *The Journal of Henry David Thoreau, 1837–1861*. New York Review Books Classics.

Tiller Foundation. (n.d.). Intention science. https://tillerfoundation.org/

Tonsager, S. (n.d.). Whisperology. www.whisperology.com

Vaidyanathan, V. (2022, July 8). What is the observer effect in quantum mechanics? *Science ABC*. https://www.scienceabc.com/pure-sciences/observer-effect-quantum-mechanics

Walsch, N. D. (2010). *When Everything Changes, Change Everything: In a Time of Turmoil, a Pathway to Peace*. Hodder Paperbacks.

Wohlleben, P. (2016). *The Hidden Life of Trees: What They Feel, Gow They Communicate*. Greystone Books.